# Anti-Audit Warfare

## *How to Avoid or Beat an IRS Audit*

From the editors of **Small Business TAX STRATEGIES**

*Contributing Advisor:* Bill Bischoff, CPA
*Editor:* Kathy A. Shipp
*Editorial Director:* Patrick DiDomenico
*Associate Publisher:* Adam Goldstein
*Publisher:* Phillip A. Ash

© 2015, 2011, 2006, 2002, 1999, 1990. Business Management Daily, a division of Capitol Information Group, 7600A Leesburg Pike, West Building, Suite 300, Falls Church, VA 22043-2004; www.BusinessManagementDaily.com. Phone: (800) 543-2055. All rights reserved. No part of this report may be reproduced in any form or by any means without written permission from the publisher. Printed in U.S.A.

ISBN: 1-880024-39-X

*This publication is designed to provide accurate and authoritative information in regard to the subject matter covered. It is sold with the understanding that the publisher is not engaged in rendering financial or legal services.*

# Contents

**Introduction: Flying Below the Audit Radar** .................................. 1
    Audit Risk Up for Many Individuals .................................. 1
    Audit Targets (and Non-Targets) .................................. 2
    Correspondence Audits vs. Field Audits .................................. 2
    Table 1: Audit Odds in Detail: 2014 vs. 2009 .................................. 3
    Learn the 'Rules of Combat' .................................. 4

**1 First Line of Defense: Your Tax Return** .................................. 5
    Arm Yourself With Good Records .................................. 5
    How Long to Retain Tax Records .................................. 5
    Table 2: Recommended Retention Periods .................................. 6
    Enlist IRS Help With Tax Questions .................................. 7
        Private letter ruling .................................. 7
        Determination letter .................................. 8
        Technical advice memorandum .................................. 8
    Don't Trust Everything the IRS Tells You .................................. 9
    If You Do Face an Audit . . . .................................. 9

**2 A Look at the IRS War Machine** .................................. 11
    IRS' First Line of Offense: Computers .................................. 12
    Second Line of Offense: The Human Touch .................................. 12
    What Raises Eyebrows? .................................. 13
    Is Your Return Waving Red Flags? .................................. 14
    Table 3: Average Deductions .................................. 15
    What Are the 'Safe' Deductions? .................................. 16
    Other Reasons for Audits .................................. 16

**3 Surviving the IRS Bullet** .................................. 19
    How to Handle the Audit Letter .................................. 19
    Three Types of Audits .................................. 19
        Correspondence audit .................................. 19
    Contact Letter From the IRS .................................. 20
    What the IRS Wants to Check .................................. 21
        Office audit .................................. 22
        Field audit .................................. 22

**4 Know Your Taxpayer Rights** .................................. 23
    Your Advocate at the IRS .................................. 23
    Liberalized Innocent-Spouse Rules .................................. 25

**5 Handling a Correspondence Audit** .................................. 27
    Negligence Penalty .................................. 27
    Example of Correspondence Audit and Resolution .................................. 28
    Sample Correspondence Audit .................................. 29

# Contents

**6 Meeting the IRS Face to Face** — 35
The IRS Is Prepared—Are You? — 35
    Battle of the bulge — 35
Should You Send a Representative? — 36
Deciding to Go It Alone — 37
Dredging Up Those Old Returns and Documents — 37
How to Reconstruct Your Records—Legally — 38
Table 4: Documents Needed to Verify Audit Items — 39
Form 2848: Power of Attorney and Declaration of Representative — 43

**7 Enduring an Office Audit** — 45
Meeting the IRS Auditor — 45
How Your Audit May End — 47

**8 Bracing for a Field Audit** — 49
Strategic Moves — 49
Hiring Professional Help — 51
Beware 'Financial-Status' Audits — 51
Be Ready to Grant a Power of Attorney — 52
    If you're targeted . . . — 53
'Good Grief! Auditors Who Really Understand My Business' — 53
Form 4549: Income Tax Examination Changes — 56

**9 Winning After Losing a Battle** — 59
Assess Your Options — 59
If You Disagree With the Adjustments . . . — 60
To Appeal or Not to Appeal . . . — 61
How to Appeal — 61
    What's so appealing? — 62
    Case closed — 63
Form 870: Waiver of Restrictions — 64
The 90-Day Letter: Notice of Deficiency — 65

**10 Taking the IRS to Court** — 67
Petitioning the Tax Court — 67
The Pros and Cons of Tax Court — 68
Other Legal Recourses — 69
To the Winner Belong Some Spoils — 69

**11 If You Lose the War** — 71
If You Don't Have the Money — 71
Can You Expect a Repeat Audit? — 71
Three Ways to Escape IRS Penalties — 72

*Introduction*

# FLYING BELOW THE AUDIT RADAR

The well-publicized IRS Restructuring and Reform Act of 1998 was intended to result in a "kinder and gentler" Internal Revenue Service. To some extent, that has happened. The law included a number of favorable and long-overdue reforms. But the IRS is still a gigantic government bureaucracy. As such, don't expect it to be as taxpayer-friendly as some members of Congress might have hoped. At the local office level in particular, progress may be grudging at best, despite generally good intentions at the national headquarters in Washington.

In addition, audit rates several years ago dropped to such low levels that it became a political embarrassment, so Congress ordered the IRS to increase audit rates and gave it bigger budgets to do so. The directive to beef up enforcement and conduct more audits then took precedence over the "kinder and gentler" concept. That said, audit rates have started falling again. The IRS blames that on tighter budgets for the last few years.

In any case, your best defense against the IRS continues to be a good offense, based on knowing how the agency works and how to take advantage of some taxpayer-friendly rules. Using the information in this special report, you'll increase your odds of easing your way through the system with less hassle while reducing your exposure to audits.

## Audit Risk Up for Many Individuals

The most recent audit statistics from the 2014 *IRS Data Book* (based on activity in the government's fiscal year ending on Sept. 30, 2014) show some trends that taxpayers should be aware of. Although the overall audit rate for individuals has remained at about 1% for the last few years, the IRS has turned up the heat over the years for higher-income individuals *(see Table 1, page 3):*

♦ Individuals with total positive income between $200,000 and $1 million were audited at a 2.2% rate in 2014, versus only .44% in 2005.

♦ Individuals with total positive income of $1 million and up were audited at a 7.5% rate in 2014, versus only .65% in 2005.

♦ Schedule C filers with gross receipts of $100,000 or more faced a 2.3% audit rate in 2014. However, the audit rate for taxpayers in this category was only 1.2% in 2001, so the IRS has turned up the heat considerably over the past decade and a half. Also, the 2.3% rate is much higher than the overall .9% rate for individuals who do not file Schedule C.

## Audit Targets (and Non-Targets)

You may turn out to be one of the unlucky "chosen" who receive an audit notice from the IRS. Even though the overall odds are still in your favor, the chances of an audit are generally higher for taxpayers with business activities (as opposed to taxpayers who earn their income from wages or investments). That said, if you have total positive income above $200,000, you face significantly higher odds of being audited regardless of your sources of income.

In contrast, if you had total positive income of less than $200,000, did not file a business tax schedule (such as Schedule C, E or F or Form 2106), and did not claim the earned income tax credit (EITC), your chance of being audited in 2014 was a microscopic .3%.

At lower income levels, claiming the earned income tax credit significantly raises the odds of being audited because the government has come to realize that the EITC is ripe for abuse. Those with total gross receipts under $25,000 who claimed the EITC faced an audit rate of 1.8% in 2014. However, the audit rate was only 1.2% in 2014 for those who claimed the EITC and had gross receipts of $25,000 or more (not so surprising because the EITC is quickly phased out as income rises).

The 2014 figures show that small C corporations (those with total assets of less than $10 million) faced an overall audit rate of only 1%. Even those with total assets between $5 million and $10 million only faced a 1.9% audit rate. Large corporations (those with total assets of more than $10 million) faced an overall audit rate of 12.2% in 2014. However, the rates quickly increased with the size of the corporation. Those with total assets between $10 million and $50 million were only audited at a 6.2% rate while those with total assets between $1 billion and $5 billion were audited at a 30.1% rate in 2014. Corporations with total assets of $20 billion or more were audited at an 84.2% rate.

Finally, your business has a much better chance of flying below the IRS audit radar if it is operated as an S corporation, partnership or multimember LLC (taxed the same as a partnership) rather than as a sole proprietorship or C corporation. The 2014 audit rates for both S corporations and entities taxed as partnerships were a mere .4% (not significantly higher than the rates in 2001). Although the IRS has repeatedly claimed it will focus more effort on auditing S corporations and entities taxed as partnerships, the numbers do not show that happening. Individuals who file Schedule F (farmers and ranchers) faced an audit rate of only .5% in 2014.

### Access the *IRS Data Book*

The IRS' annual *Data Book* provides a wealth of information for taxpayers to ponder, including the percentage of returns audited, the amount of tax revenue collected, the number of tax refunds, and figures on electronic filing. It also features state-by-state breakdowns in categories ranging from types of returns filed, to audit percentages and collections.

You can access all the IRS' *Data Books,* dating back to fiscal year 2000, online at **www.irs.gov/taxstats** (click on "IRS Data Books" in the Products, Publications & Papers section). Or, you can request copies by calling the U.S. Government Publishing Office at (866) 512-1800.

## INTRODUCTION

### Table 1: Audit Odds in Detail: 2014 vs. 2009

| Taxpayer Category | Audit Rate (%) 2014 | Audit Rate (%) 2009 |
|---|---|---|
| *Individuals—Nonbusiness* | | |
| Total gross receipts under $25,000 with earned income tax credit claimed | 1.8 | 2.2 |
| Total gross receipts of $25,000 or more with earned income tax credit claimed | 1.2 | 1.8 |
| Total positive income of less than $200,000 | 0.3 | 0.4 |
| Total positive income of less than $200,000 with Schedule E (rental income) or Form 2106 (employee business expenses) | 0.7 | 1.3 |
| Total positive income of $200,000 to $1 million | 2.2 | 2.3 |
| Total positive income of $1 million or more | 7.5 | 6.4 |
| *Individuals—With Schedule C Gross Receipts of* | | |
| $25,000 to $100,000 | 1.9 | 1.9 |
| $100,000 or more | 2.3 | 3.7 |
| *C Corporations—With Assets of* | | |
| Under $250,000 | 0.8 | 0.7 |
| $250,000 to $1 million | 1.2 | 1.3 |
| $1 million to $5 million | 1.2 | 1.8 |
| $5 million to $10 million | 1.9 | 2.7 |
| $10 million to $50 million | 6.2 | 10.1 |
| $50 million to $100 million | 11.2 | 14.3 |
| $100 million to $250 million | 13.1 | 13.6 |
| $250 million or more | 26.1 | 25.7 |
| *S Corporations* | 0.4 | 0.4 |
| *Partnerships and Multimember LLCs* | 0.4 | 0.4 |

Source: IRS Data Book, 2014, 2009

## Correspondence Audits vs. Field Audits

Thankfully, most IRS audits of individual taxpayers are so-called correspondence audits; you simply receive a written notice about some perceived tax return issues and are asked to respond in writing. Correspondence audits are far less intimidating than so-called field audits, where you (or your tax pro) are required to meet with an auditor face-to-face at the local IRS office or, even worse, at your place of business or home.

According to the IRS data:

♦ In 2014, 71% of total audits were of the correspondence variety.
♦ For individuals with total positive income below $200,000, and with no business tax forms (Schedules C, E, F or Form 2106) and no earned income tax

credit claimed, 86% of audits were correspondence audits in 2014 (versus 90% in 2009).
- For individuals with total positive income below $200,000 with business tax forms (Schedules C, E, F or Form 2106) but no earned income tax credit claimed, 52% were correspondence audits in 2014 (versus 69% in 2009). However, for income between $100,000 and $200,000, 75% of audits were the more daunting field audits. This apparently reflects an increased emphasis on field audits for middle-income Schedule C filers.
- For individuals with total positive income between $200,000 and $1 million, 73% of audits were of the correspondence variety in 2014 as long as no business tax forms were included in the return (about the same as in 2009).
- For individuals with total positive income between $200,000 and $1 million *and* business tax forms included in the return, the correspondence audits rate was 55% in 2014. The other 45% faced the more daunting field audits (about the same as in 2009).
- For individuals with total positive income above $1 million (from whatever sources), the correspondence audit rate in 2014 was 56%. The other 44% faced field audits.

In contrast to the situation for individual taxpayers, the vast majority of audits of business entities (corporations, partnerships and LLCs) are field audits: 92% of C corporation audits were field audits in 2014; 91% of S corporation audits (what few there were) and 67% of partnership audits were field audits.

## Learn the 'Rules of Combat'

Once you finish reading this special report and apply some of our "Rules of Combat," your audit odds may improve to the point of being better than 111 to 1 (the overall audit rate for individual taxpayers). This report will advise you on how to fly under the radar screen and maintain a low tax profile. Dealing with the IRS is comparable to warfare: Some of its examiners "take no prisoners" and might continue to adopt unreasonable stances despite recent reforms to prevent this practice.

Take the case of a lawyer who had been audited 12 times in 27 years. He finally had enough and sued for relief in a U.S. District Court. The lawyer claimed he had no tax shelters, his fees were his only income, and the IRS had never found he owed more than what he'd paid. One auditor told him that the IRS computers picked him out because of his lack of deductions. An auditor-trainee, however, admitted that he persisted in asking for documents so that he would look diligent to his supervisors.

That case should rid you of the belief that you're randomly selected for an audit. That's not true in most cases. You'll see this after reading about how your tax return is scrutinized, first by IRS computers and then by agency personnel. In the event that you're one of those targeted, we'll show you how to shore up your arsenal of defenses for a showdown with the IRS.

# First Line of Defense: Your Tax Return 1

Because you're vulnerable to the IRS through your tax return, the first lesson is to make the return as impregnable as possible. This means not only putting your best facts and figures forward when it comes to income, losses, deductions and exemptions but also buttressing them with documentation. (In Section 2, "A Look at the IRS War Machine," we'll cover in detail the steps to filing "audit-proof" returns.)

Legally, the IRS has three years to audit your return (six if your return understates gross income by more than 25%). In other words, generally the agency can assess additional tax on a return only during the three years after the date you filed the return or the due date, whichever is later. Fortunately, the agency just doesn't have the manpower to pore over returns that are more than two years old unless some special circumstance warrants it.

*Rule of Combat No. 1:* Unless the IRS selects your return for audit within two years of the filing date, you're probably home free.

## Arm Yourself With Good Records

In relying on your tax return to head off IRS troubles, your first line of defense will be the underlying documents. Refer to page 39 for the types of materials you'll need to support particular tax items that the IRS might question, such as exemptions, medical expenses, state and local taxes, contributions, casualty losses and business expenses.

The tax laws and regulations give the IRS the general authority to require taxpayers to maintain records to support their federal income tax returns. Everyone who's subject to income taxes or is required to file income tax returns should keep permanent books of account and sufficient records to establish the amounts of income, deductions, credits or other items shown on the return. (However, farmers and wage earners aren't required to keep formal books of account. They simply need to keep or supply to their employers sufficient records that allow the IRS to determine taxable income correctly in the event of an audit.)

## How Long to Retain Tax Records

As a rule, you must keep books and records as long as the information may be "material in the administration of the income tax laws." For practical purposes, this means keeping them for as long as there's a possibility the taxpayer could file an amended return or a refund claim or the IRS could audit the return or assess additional tax.

As noted, the IRS generally has *three* years after a return is filed to assess additional tax. However, it has *no* limitation period on assessing additional taxes in the following situations: if no return is filed; if the return is false or fraudulent; or if the individual made a willful attempt to evade tax. If a person omits more than 25% of gross income from the return, the IRS can assess additional tax at any time within six years of the return's filing.

For tax credits or refunds, you must file a claim for credit or a refund within three years of filing the return or *two* years from the time the tax was paid, whichever comes later.

**Bottom line:** Books and records relating to income tax returns should be kept a minimum of three years from the date you filed the return. It probably makes sense to keep records proving reported income amounts (bank statements, 1099s, etc.) for at least six years to head off any IRS claim that you omitted more than 25% of gross income.

You should keep the tax returns themselves forever to prove that you filed them. Underlying financial records—such as annual business financial statements and reconciliations to tax returns—probably should be kept indefinitely to overcome any IRS assertion that tax returns were false or fraudulent or you made a willful attempt to evade taxes.

In summary, the document retention periods shown in Table 2 are general guidelines. In some cases, the retention period recommended may be for nontax reasons; for example, real estate records should be kept forever to prove ownership and for environmental-liability exposure reasons.

## Table 2: Recommended Retention Periods

| Type of Record | Retention Period |
| --- | --- |
| Copies of tax returns as filed | Forever |
| Tax and legal correspondence | Forever |
| Audit reports | Forever |
| General ledger and journals | Forever |
| Financial statements | Forever |
| Contracts and leases | Forever |
| Real estate records | Forever |
| Corporate stock records and minutes | Forever |
| Bank statements and deposit slips | 6 years* |
| Sales records and journals | 6 years* |
| Other records relating to revenue | 6 years* |
| Employee expense reports and records relating to travel and entertainment expenses | 6 years* |
| Canceled checks | 3 years* |
| Paid vendor invoices | 3 years* |
| Employee payroll expense records | 3 years* |
| Inventory records | 3 years** |
| Depreciation schedules | At least tax life of asset plus 3 years |
| Other capital asset records | At least tax life of asset plus 3 years |
| Other records relating to expenses | 3 years* |

\* From the later of the tax return due date or filing date.
\*\* Forever if you use the last in, first out (LIFO) method.

# Enlist IRS Help With Tax Questions

If you hit a stumbling block about tax law when making out your return, you may want to consider applying for a **private ruling**: i.e., one that applies to your particular situation. In other words, you can ask the IRS for its approval, or disapproval, in advance of something you propose to do. This may help you avoid later IRS questions and a possible audit. Private rulings fall into three categories: **private letter rulings, determination letters** and **technical advice memoranda**. Each can be useful for tax issues that fall into gray areas of the law.

## *Private letter ruling*

You can use a private letter ruling (PLR) to find out how the IRS will treat a proposed transaction (or, less likely, one you've already completed). These rulings affect only the taxpayers to whom they are issued, so technically others can't use them except as general guidance and an indication of where the IRS stands on an issue. They can't be used in court as a controlling authority, nor technically do they bind the IRS to rule the same way if the issue comes up again. Nevertheless, private letter rulings issued over a period of time give you a strong indication of IRS policy on particular tax law questions. Also, they can be used in administrative proceedings (such as when you appeal an audit finding that you owe more tax) to support your position and even in the courts as an indication of IRS practice.

Taxpayers can also use rulings issued to others to help rebut government penalty assessments for negligence and/or intentional disregard of the tax rules and regulations. Moreover, the rulings can serve as the "substantial authority" needed to avoid the 20% penalty on relatively large understatements of tax.

For example, you might ask for your own PLR when there's doubt about how the tax laws would apply to a major transaction and when the potential negative tax impact could be heavy. A PLR might also be appropriate when you want to be sure of the tax consequences of a move you plan to make in the near future. You shouldn't ask for a ruling on a subject that the IRS has said it will not rule on, such as the useful life of an asset or whether compensation is reasonable in a specific case.

*Caution:* If you're taking a radically different approach from IRS policy or prior rulings, a private letter ruling probably won't help you much and almost certainly will tell you something you don't want to hear. Even though your position may be supportable, there's no point in asking for IRS approval when you plan to take a very aggressive stance.

➤ **Recommendation:** Don't ask for a ruling if you don't want to draw the IRS' attention. More important, don't ask and then withdraw your request if you get an indication from the IRS that its ruling won't be in your favor. You won't be bound by the finding the ruling would have presented, but it may increase your chances of being audited. The IRS generally will notify your local district office that you have requested a ruling and have withdrawn your request. In its communiqué, the IRS will inform the district office about the issue you requested a ruling on and the tax years involved.

In many cases, you're better off simply locating a private letter ruling issued to another taxpayer about the same tricky issue you're now facing. Or, you might consider buying a software product suitable for hard-core "do-it-yourself" taxpayers. The OneDisc DVD from the nonprofit publisher Tax Analysts includes the texts of most of the PLRs issued since 1980. Using the software, you can do a keyword search for PLRs on your subject. Although intended for tax professionals, OneDisc is useful for anyone who's not about to be intimidated by a mass of government verbiage. OneDisc includes IRS Market Segment Specialization Program (MSSP) guides, which are intended to train auditors about tax issues to look for in specific industries. As explained on page 53, these guides can be helpful sources of information for taxpayers as well. For more information on OneDisc, call Tax Analysts at (800) 955-3444 or go to **www.taxanalysts.com**.

If you finally decide to go ahead with your own PLR, you'll probably need professional help in drafting the required submission to the IRS. The details are set forth in a "revenue procedure," which spells out the information you must supply and the protocol for requesting a ruling from the IRS' national headquarters. Unfortunately, the drill is complicated enough to keep a tax pro busy for days—at a price, of course.

Then you have to pay a federal "user fee" of $500 if your personal gross income is less than $250,000 ($6,000 if it's higher). For business-related tax questions, the fee is $500 for taxpayers with gross income under $1 million and $6,000 for those with gross income of $1 million or more. The IRS has ruled that the cost of getting a private letter ruling is deductible. Both the fee paid to a tax practitioner to prepare a ruling request on a nonbusiness transaction and the user fee paid to the IRS are miscellaneous itemized deductions. In the case of a business tax issue, you should be able to fully deduct these expenses as business write-offs.

Shortly after you make your request, the IRS usually will tell you informally how it's going to rule. As we have pointed out, in the event the IRS indicates an adverse ruling, you can withdraw the request—but with consequences. But if the IRS rules in your favor, it won't go back on the ruling, except in rare cases.

## *Determination letter*

Generally, you would use a determination letter to seek approval of items such as an individually designed pension, a stock bonus or a profit-sharing plan. You also might use one to obtain approval for the tax-exempt status of an organization. To request a determination letter, contact the IRS district office that has audit jurisdiction over the transaction or the business entity involved. With a letter in hand, you'll be prepared if a revenue agent raises questions about the validity of your plan or operation.

## *Technical advice memorandum*

Technical advice memoranda (TAMs) are helpful when you're being audited and aren't satisfied with the tax law interpretations you received from the IRS. Request that the auditor seek a TAM. Basically, the only differences between a TAM and a PLR are that an IRS employee initiates a request for a TAM and you won't pay a user fee. Also, PLRs are usually made in advance of major transactions while TAMs deal with tax questions related to "done deals." A TAM is most useful when the issue involves confusing or conflicting tax laws, or when IRS positions on the subject are inconsistent. Note also that the request for advice will suspend your audit issue until the national office sends its determination. If the agent thinks he's on shaky ground, your request for a TAM may even force a full-fledged retreat.

## Don't Trust Everything the IRS Tells You

Be cautious about advice from the IRS other than in PLRs. Court records are filled with cases in which the taxpayer claimed to have received specific advice from an IRS office. It's an unfortunate fact of the tax laws that relying on bad advice from the government simply doesn't get you off the hook in any way, shape or form. Be especially wary of telephone advice. Surveys over the years indicate that IRS telephone advice on tax issues can be wrong an alarming number of times.

What about IRS publications? Generally, they're helpful, but they can be wrong, too. Take the case of Richard Gnyp, whose business had a net operating loss in 1974. He deducted the loss on his 1981 tax return by relying on the advice of his accountant and IRS Publication 334 (*Tax Guide for Small Business*). The publication mistakenly stated that the pre-1976 carryover period for losses was seven years. In fact, the period was five years.

The IRS tried to correct its error with a public announcement in March 1982, but Gnyp and his accountant never got the word. That's too bad, the Tax Court later said. The IRS corrected its error well before Gnyp filed his return. It wasn't the revenue agency's fault that he didn't get the message (and although the court didn't say so, it actually would have made no difference if the IRS had failed even to try to fix the mistake).

Gnyp's misplaced reliance on his accountant and the IRS publication weren't enough to save the day, the court said, as it upheld assessment of a tax deficiency against him. (*Gnyp v. Commissioner*, T.C. Memo 1988-488, Docket No. 39928-86) Unfortunately, the result wouldn't be any different today, even since passage of the IRS Restructuring and Reform Act.

*Rule of Combat No. 2:* Make sure any advice you receive from the IRS is in writing. Why? Because the agency must abate any part of a penalty or extra tax that's caused by inaccurate written advice it gave you. Keep the written advice with the tax records for that year's return.

## If You Do Face an Audit . . .

If, despite your best efforts to file returns safe from IRS scrutiny, you're notified of a forthcoming audit, don't panic. The rest of this special report offers plenty of strategies about what you should do. But here's some advance advice, right off the top.

Understand that the IRS generally has a limited game plan and will follow it—unless you do something that encourages the auditor to expand her scope. You should receive a notice showing which items are under scrutiny. Now your job is simply to provide support for what you did on your return. Be polite. Auditors have the right to expect courteous, professional treatment from you. And they can make your life miserable if they want to—so don't give them any reasons. Provide the specific data requested, and give only succinct answers to direct questions.

Everything should relate strictly to your return *as you filed it*. In other words, don't volunteer information.

If the queries start to head off toward "lifestyle issues" (such as how you paid for your house and cars), you may be under a so-called financial-status audit (*see Section 8, "Bracing for a Field Audit"*). The auditor is looking for unreported income, which is cause for concern. At this point, you may need a professional to represent you.

Also, if you think you can't properly prepare for an audit or are uncomfortable about facing the auditor, consider hiring a tax pro to represent you. This can be expensive, but it may be well worth it. Usually, your representative can stand in your place, and you may not even have to appear at any meetings. Generally, you also can arrange for the auditor to do her work at your representative's office. That keeps her out of your home or business, where what she sees and hears can lead to even more questions. Competent tax pros are good at forcing the IRS to stick to the program and get the matter resolved. Some are gifted at finding deductions you missed and favorable tax rules you didn't consider in filing your return. These can be traded off against items the IRS finds that would result in underpayments.

Finally, don't insist on "total victory" even if you think you were right about everything. Your time is valuable. Give the auditor a few small wins so that she can report some favorable statistics and close out the case. Then you can resume your normal routine without the distraction of an ongoing IRS dispute.

# A Look at the IRS War Machine 2

To understand the IRS operation, let's briefly look at the journey your tax return takes after you file it. The agency's process helps determine whom it will audit. Your return is sent to your regional IRS service center, where it's sorted according to (1) whether it represents a business or personal tax accounting and (2) the type of filing status (i.e., married filing jointly or separately, or single). IRS personnel then compare the return and the accompanying check if tax is due. Then they code the information and input your tax return data into their computer system.

Once your return hits the computer, it undergoes rigorous and speedy checks for mathematical errors and other mistakes in preparing the return.

*Rule of Combat No. 3:* Although the absence of obvious mistakes (such as math errors or missing forms) on your return means a lower tax profile for you, don't get upset if you make errors like this. They won't cause your return to be singled out for an audit.

An obviously deficient return may generate a notice from the feds, but you will be given a chance to correct these types of problems without drawing further attention.

In contrast, audits are largely meant to "scare" people into compliance, as well as to make money for the government. Plus, you can get into an audit situation by disagreeing with the IRS on how to interpret specific tax rules. Once the audit door is opened, it's open all the way. The government can examine every aspect of your return; it need not limit the process to the original issue.

*Rule of Combat No. 4:* Don't challenge the IRS on tax law interpretations unless your position is solid and the dollars involved in the disputed issue are large in relation to the dollar "exposure" caused by other possibly questionable areas of your tax return.

Once you challenge the agency on tax law, your return most likely will be sent to a district or local office, and you'll be invited to explain your position in person. It's at this stage when you may be giving an IRS examiner an invitation to launch a full-blown audit of your entire return.

## IRS' First Line of Offense: Computers

Computers have become the IRS' best weapon, or the taxpayer's worst enemy, depending on your point of view. In other words, the computer process enables the agency to cross-check or match information quickly on a return not only with data about you from other sources but also with "average" returns. For instance, much of the information on Form 1099, which reports interest and dividends paid to you by banks and brokerages as well as fees from consulting and freelance work, is forwarded to the IRS electronically, so the agency can quickly cross-check the accuracy of the information you include on your return.

Traditionally, the IRS has used computers to plug your tax return figures into its mathematical scoring system, known as the Discriminate Index Function (DIF), which rates the probability of inaccurate information on returns. A few years ago, the agency launched another audit selection tool, the Unreported Income Discriminate Index Formula (UIDIF), which systematically identifies returns at high risk for unreported income. Now all tax returns receive a UIDIF score as well as a DIF score.

Of all returns audited, 75% to 80% are selected via the computer's DIF system. The remainder are selected through various IRS programs, such as ones targeting specific industries and occupations and large tax-refund claims.

*Rule of Combat No. 5: Be sure your return includes all income reported on "information returns," such as Forms W-2 and 1099. Amounts on information returns are reported to the government, and IRS computer matching programs will almost surely single out your return if anything is missing. If you have a good reason to omit an amount (for example, you actually received the income in the following tax year), include the number in your return as gross income, then use a separate line to "back it out" as a negative amount with an appropriate explanation.*

## Second Line of Offense: The Human Touch

Once the computer flags a return, humans may enter the process to search for reasons why figures may not conform to averages. Returns that are prime candidates for an audit are forwarded to district offices. IRS personnel, called classifiers, pore over them to examine the audit points flagged by computer.

Here's where the human touch is needed: Although the computer can spot figures that don't fall within certain average ranges, it obviously can't read statements or evaluate any additional information filed with the return to explain the figure in question. For instance, computers may have singled out a return for its unusually large amount of medical expense deductions. On closer inspection, however, the IRS employee may find that the taxpayer is age 65 or older, thus belonging to a category of citizens who incur above-average medical expenses. Also, the taxpayer may have attached copies of receipts or statements explaining those medical expenses, which a human can spot but a computer can't.

***Rule of Combat No. 6:*** *Cover yourself with documentation. At this stage of the return-processing function, documentation is especially important and may determine whether you get an IRS visit or a call. Include all required IRS schedules and forms in your return. Also, enclose any statement that proves your tax point, especially on matters that are sure to raise IRS eyebrows. You may be able to save yourself from an audit if the classifier is satisfied with your evidence or proof. This may include photocopies of canceled checks or copies of legal documents (such as a divorce decree to prove claimed alimony deductions).*

## What Raises Eyebrows?

Basically, classifiers look for items that seem out of kilter with the averages and for which the tax return provides no obvious explanation.

In any given year, returns coming out of various geographical regions can reflect expenses or other figures that don't fall within computer averages but that taxpayers can justify. For instance, taxpayers can be expected to have unusually large casualty losses and medical expenses to report in locales that have been declared federal disaster areas after, say, a hurricane or a flood.

District offices have their own peculiarities. They're not confined to examining only the items that the computer has flagged. Each office emphasizes its own tax issues. It may, for example, look more closely at returns with an office in the home or for businesses in particular local industries known to have many tax issues.

Similarly, the classifier may focus on a particular type of tax return discrepancy that he's found to produce good results—in terms of additional tax payments. It may have nothing to do with the flagged item. In other words, once the return reaches the hands of the classifier, it becomes fair game.

Almost all classifiers will check certain points. Among them:

- **Make sure your reported income** seems sufficient to support your claimed exemptions and deductions. If you have a considerable number of exemptions, for example, a small amount of reported income could indicate to the classifier that you have another, unreported source of income.
- **Note that large refunds** are somewhat suspect in and of themselves because taxpayers typically don't put themselves in the position of prepaying more taxes than they'll end up owing for the year.
- **Be particularly careful** if you're in an occupation in which you must voluntarily report income to an employer: for example, waiting tables or styling hair. The IRS may tend to assume you have underreported tips or other income. Keep in mind that tax must be paid on income when it's earned. That's the reason for filing estimated tax payments on a quarterly basis to cover nonwage income.
- **Be especially cautious** if you're in a profession or a line of business that generates a high income. For example, the IRS becomes suspicious of a doctor whose

return reflects only marginal profitability. In general, the IRS expects most physicians to make, and report, a healthy profit.
- **If you're in business** for yourself, itemize your deductions on the business schedule (Schedule C). Beware if you don't. Those businesspeople who report high gross income from the business, show a small profit and take the standard deduction on their personal returns are waving a red flag in front of an IRS classifier. There's a tendency to believe that they are "burying" non-deductible personal expenses in the business write-off numbers.
- **Although the IRS permits** you to round off some figures to the nearest dollar, don't round off deductions to the nearest hundred or thousand. Why? Round numbers make it appear you're "guesstimating" the figure, which is sure to raise IRS eyebrows. Exact figures on a return appear to be taken from records.

*Caution:* If you're self-employed with relatively high gross income, the IRS has you in its sights. Don't trigger an audit by being sloppy. Keep a low profile by making sure you report everything shown on Forms 1099 (including interest and dividends). Failure to do this is tantamount to begging for an audit. You're also a target if you hire independent contractors: Be prepared to prove they aren't actually employees for whom you should be coughing up payroll taxes.

## Is Your Return Waving Red Flags?

If so, your chances of risking an audit may be higher. Some red flags are unavoidable. You generally should claim all the deductions you're entitled to. Just make sure your recordkeeping is rock-solid.

Here are some common red-flag items:

**Big T&E Write-Offs.** Nothing has changed here, even though meal and entertainment expenses now are only 50% deductible. The IRS knows that many taxpayers will still try to write off personal expenses as business costs. Follow the three R's to avoid problems: recordkeeping, recordkeeping and recordkeeping.

**Depreciating "Listed Property."** Some equipment with legitimate business uses also can also be used for personal reasons. Some examples are cars, home computers, televisions, camcorders, VCRs and photographic equipment. You need records showing business rather than personal usage. In particular, classifiers are on the lookout for depreciation of "luxury cars." Know the limits on the amount you can depreciate each year for business use, regardless of how much you paid for the car. Some taxpayers are claiming more than the allowable amount of depreciation in the first year. Others are overstating the business-use percentage, which results in overstated deductions.

**High Interest Expense on Individual Returns.** Because personal interest is no longer deductible at all and investment interest is deductible only to the extent of investment income, taxpayers have started "moving things around" to beat the system. For example, they may try to write off personal car loan interest by plopping it on Schedule C, or they may describe credit card interest as investment interest. *This poisons the water for all taxpayers.* If you have substantial deductible interest expense other than from your mortgage (which is generally reported to the government on information returns), be ready to prove it.

**Unreported Income Shown on Information Returns.** Don't even think about failing to report income shown on W-2s and 1099s. Your odds of getting away with it are poor and you may trigger a full-fledged audit of everything on your return. It's just not worth it.

**Unusually High Itemized Deductions.** If you claim unusually large deductions for someone in your income category, the IRS computer may spit out your tax return for a closer look. It might even lead to an audit.

That doesn't mean you should back away from deducting perfectly legitimate expenses on your tax return. But if you're way above the national averages shown in Table 3, be prepared to substantiate those deductions.

The latest averages, recently released by the IRS, relate to 2011 tax returns and take into account only taxpayers who claimed the specific deductions on their returns.

### Table 3: Average Deductions

| AGI | Interest | Taxes | Charitable donations | Medical expenses |
|---|---|---|---|---|
| **$50,000-$99,999** | $ 8,768 | $ 6,235 | $ 2,881 | $ 7,375 |
| **$100,000-$199,999** | 11,266 | 10,852 | 3,889 | 10,002 |
| **$200,000-$249,999** | 15,216 | 18,083 | 5,703 | 16,814 |
| **$250,000 & above** | 20,685 | 47,616 | 18,490 | 34,796 |

*Source:* IRS Statistics of Income 2011 Data

**High Miscellaneous Deductions.** To avoid the 2% of AGI floor on itemized deductions, some taxpayers are improperly shifting these expenses to Schedule C (Profit or Loss From a Business) or Schedule F (Farm Income and Expenses). Be sure to categorize your miscellaneous deductions rather than simply listing the total dollar amount for "miscellaneous." You can take care of this by spelling out the type of deduction—investment counsel fees, safe-deposit box rental and so on—on the dotted lines to the left of the column containing the total dollar amount.

**Losses From Sideline Businesses.** The IRS is going after some businesses that rack up tax losses year after year by trying to characterize them as nondeductible "hobbies." Under the so-called hobby loss rules, you can deduct expenses only to the extent of income from the activity. In other words, you can't generate an overall tax loss from the activity. However, if your sideline business earns at least some profit in three out of five consecutive years (two out of seven for raising horses), generally you can escape this categorization.

**Early Retirement Plan Distributions.** Taxpayers with distributions from qualified retirement plans (pension and profit-sharing plans, including self-employed plans) and individual retirement accounts (IRAs) before age 59½ are generally subject to a 10% early-withdrawal penalty tax (except if they're disabled, the distribution is due to the taxpayer's death, or benefits are paid out as an annuity over the remaining life expectancy). Some taxpayers are reporting their early distributions as taxable income, but they aren't fessing up to the 10% penalty tax (figured on Form 5329).

*Note:* The 10% premature-withdrawal penalty tax doesn't apply to IRA withdrawals used to cover qualified educational expenses, certain home-buying expenses and unreimbursed medical expenses in excess of 10% of AGI, or to unemployed persons who use IRA withdrawals for medical insurance premiums.

---

### What Are the 'Safe' Deductions?

To avoid problems in the event of an audit, treat all deductions the same: that is, make sure you can back them up with documentation. No deductions are completely safe, but some are safer than others.

Rarely will you trigger an audit for items such as mortgage interest, real estate taxes, state income tax, exemptions for your own children, union and professional dues, and the costs of professional journals, drugs and medical expenses, safe-deposit boxes and tax preparation.

Items that are more likely to draw the attention of IRS examiners but don't really meet the "red-flag" definition are deductions for the following:

- Casualty losses
- Relatively large charitable contributions of noncash property
- Losses from rentals of vacation homes
- Bad-debt losses

Needless to say, if your return contains such items, be sure to fill out the forms correctly and completely, and attach any required statements or documentation to your return to avoid the headache of being called into your local IRS office to prove your case. Note that in the event of casualty losses, taxpayers often compute the deduction incorrectly.

---

***Rule of Combat No. 7:*** *Although filing amended tax returns is perfectly legal, it does call IRS attention to your return, especially if you're asking for a refund because you "forgot" to include a deduction on your original return. The IRS reasons that if you forgot one item, you may have forgotten several more. Therefore, it may pay to take another (harder) look at your return.*

## Other Reasons for Audits

Besides having your return flagged by an IRS computer, a number of circumstances make taxpayers attractive as audit candidates.

In other words, regardless of DIF scores, you stand a higher chance of facing an audit if:

- Your income is $200,000 or more a year.
- Your gross income is $100,000–$200,000, but you show only $50,000 in taxable income.
- You file two or more Schedules C (business) or F (farm) in one year and report total losses of $25,000 or more.

The reason for targeting these "heavy hitters" is simple: The IRS has a good statistical chance of collecting bigger payoffs when their returns contain errors.

When you know the IRS has you in its sights, the implications are easy to understand. Be prepared to back up your claimed deductions with good records, and make sure the tax return itself is complete, accurate and neat.

# Surviving the IRS Bullet     3

Let's assume you are the 1 in 111th taxpayer who's hit with an audit. You find this out when you receive a "contact letter" from your friends at the IRS.

Say you were careful in filling out your return, reported all your income, took only legitimate deductions and have the documentation to prove your numbers. In this case, the fact you've received a letter is only an indication that the agency has selected your return because it doesn't fall within the norms. It doesn't mean that the IRS examiner will make adjustments. In fact, many audited returns result in no change. Some taxpayers even get refunds when they realize, upon further review, that they overlooked deductible items or favorable special rules.

## How to Handle the Audit Letter

The IRS letter will spell out what the agency requires from you. It will indicate which items or issues on your return have been "classified," or selected, for audit. Generally, it lists two to three issues, and these are the only items you must support with documentation to avoid paying any additional tax.

The contact letter also will tell you how long you have to respond before the IRS simply adjusts your tax in its favor, usually 30 days. After you've assembled all your documentation, respond promptly.

To resolve the issues raised by the government, the letter will ask you to mail in your receipts, call for an appointment or come to the IRS office at a time set forth in the letter. *(See the sample letter on page 20.)*

With your letter you should also receive copies of IRS Notice 609, "Privacy Act Notice"; IRS Publication 1, *Your Rights As a Taxpayer*; and IRS Publication 5, *Your Appeal Rights and How to Prepare a Protest If You Don't Agree.*

## Three Types of Audits

In effect, the contact letter also lets you know which of the three types of examinations the IRS will conduct. (In Sections 5, 7 and 8, we'll walk you through the minefields that can arise in each type of audit.)

### *Correspondence audit*

The **correspondence or mail audit** is the least threatening and, by far, the most common. In handling this type of examination, you'll probably never see an IRS employee. The entire matter is handled through an exchange of letters and documentation. Such examinations are generally limited to a few items or issues that you can easily prove by mailing copies of bills, checks, receipts or other relevant documents. Frequently, the auditor wants to check only a deduction that's larger than those usually taken by people in your income category.

If, for example, you have large itemized deductions compared with your income, you'll probably be asked to back them up. Or you may be asked to explain why

*(continued on page 22)*

# Contact Letter From the IRS

The following is a sample of what an IRS "contact letter" will look like when your return is selected for an audit. The reverse side (*see next page*) specifies the areas the IRS wants to check.

---

**Internal Revenue Service**  Department of the Treasury
District Director

                                   Person to Contact:
                                   Telephone Number:
                                   Date:

    Your Federal income tax return has been selected for examination. On the reverse side please see the specific items to be examined for the tax year(s) shown below. It is very important that you contact our office within 10 days from the date on this letter. Please call the number shown above to arrange an appointment. For your convenience, the following space is provided to record the appointment:

    Tax Year(s):                              Date:
    Place:                                        Day:
    Room No.:                              Time:

    If you filed a joint return, either you or your spouse may keep the appointment. You may also authorize someone else to represent you by completing Form 2848, Power of Attorney and Declaration of Representative.

    Please bring this letter with you to the interview. Also bring the complete records needed to verify the items checked. Without the requested records, we will have to proceed on the basis of available information. Your cooperation is, therefore, essential.

    Enclosed is Notice 782, Information on Tax Examinations, which briefly explains the examination process and your appeal rights. If you have any questions, please contact the person shown above.

                                               Sincerely,

                                           District Director

Enclosures:
Notice 609
Notice 782
Publication 1
                                                (over)

District Director, Manhattan District              **Letter 2203(DO) (Rev. 10-88)**

# What the IRS Wants to Check

The back page of the agency's audit notice lists the items being audited on your return. These are the only items you must support with documentation.

---

Please bring records to support the following items reported on your tax return for _____.

- ❏ Alimony Payments or Income
- ❏ Automobile Expenses
- ❏ Bad Debts
- ❏ Capital Gains and Losses
- ❏ Casualty Losses
- ❏ Contributions
- ❏ Credit for Child and Dependent Care Expenses
- ❏ Education Expenses
- ❏ Employee Business Expenses

- ❏ Energy Credit
- ❏ Exemptions (Child/Children, Other)
- ❏ Filing Status
- ❏ Income
- ❏ Interest Expense
- ❏ Medical and Dental Expenses
- ❏ Miscellaneous Deductions
- ❏ Moving Expenses
- ❏ Rental Income and Expenses

- ❏ Sale or Exchange of Residence
- ❏ Taxes
- ❏ Uniform, Equipment, and Tools
- ❏ Copy of your Federal tax return(s) for _____
- ❏ _____
- ❏ _____
- ❏ _____
- ❏ _____
- ❏ _____

**Schedule C**

- ❏ All Business Expenses
- ❏ Bad Debts
- ❏ Car and Truck Expense
- ❏ Commissions
- ❏ Cost of Goods Sold
- ❏ Depreciation
- ❏ _____

- ❏ Gross Receipts
- ❏ Insurance
- ❏ Interest
- ❏ Legal and Professional
- ❏ Rent
- ❏ Repairs
- ❏ _____

- ❏ Salaries and Wages
- ❏ Supplies
- ❏ Taxes
- ❏ Travel and Entertainment
- ❏ _____
- ❏ _____
- ❏ _____

**Schedule F**

- ❏ All Farm Expenses
- ❏ Depreciation
- ❏ Feed Purchased
- ❏ Fertilizers and Lime
- ❏ Gross Receipts
- ❏ _____

- ❏ Insurance
- ❏ Inventories
- ❏ Labor Hired
- ❏ Machine Hire
- ❏ Other Farm Income
- ❏ _____

- ❏ Repairs and Maintenance
- ❏ Supplies Purchased
- ❏ Taxes
- ❏ _____
- ❏ _____
- ❏ _____

**Letter 2203(DO)(Rev. 10-88)**

*(continued from page 19)*

income reported on a Form 1099 wasn't included in your return. You may have simply missed an item or inadvertently combined it with another income item in the return. Or you may have a good reason for not reporting any taxable income, such as a retirement plan distribution being rolled over tax free into your IRA.

In any case, the IRS is just looking for an explanation and/or some additional tax dollars with a correspondence audit. Generally, this kind of audit is easy to resolve in a reasonable manner.

## *Office audit*

The **office or desk audit** is what you'll face if the letter from the IRS gives an appointment time and asks you to bring certain records and other information to the auditor's office.

The IRS policy guide lists the issues that are covered in an office audit. They may include income from tips, pensions, annuities, rents, royalties, second jobs, capital gains and losses, deductions for employees' business expenses, complex casualty and theft losses and bad debts.

## *Field audit*

During a **field audit** the IRS auditor comes to your business office (or sometimes your home) or to your tax advisor's office, if that's where you keep all your books and records.

This kind of examination is more extensive than the other audit types and is generally reserved for businesses, individuals with large and complex returns, or cases where the IRS suspects significant tax dollars have been underpaid (perhaps because of unreported income).

# KNOW YOUR TAXPAYER RIGHTS 4

Before we advise you on how to handle the three types of audits explained in Section 3, you should be aware of the Taxpayer Bill of Rights, the more recent Taxpayer Bill of Rights 2 legislation, as well as favorable changes included in the IRS Restructuring and Reform Act of 1998. Because taxpayers have voiced so many complaints about the IRS' tactics over the years, Congress finally passed laws giving taxpayers more protection against wrongful or unreasonable behavior by the IRS and its personnel. Here are some of the key provisions in those laws.

**You have a statutory right** to appoint someone to represent you in IRS proceedings. Generally, you can't be forced to attend interviews with agents as long as your representative (CPA, attorney or Enrolled Agent) adheres to the requirements of the law. To engage a representative, you must fill out Form 2848 (Power of Attorney and Declaration of Representative). *See sample on page 43.*

**Before starting an audit** or collection interview with you, an agent must explain your rights, including your right to suspend the interview to consult with your tax advisor, even if you haven't formally appointed him as your representative.

**The agency must abate** any part of a penalty or extra tax that is caused by inaccurate *written* advice the IRS gave you.

---

### Your Advocate at the IRS

The IRS Restructuring and Reform Act of 1998 established the position of the "national taxpayer advocate," who is appointed by the Secretary of the Treasury and need not be a career IRS employee. The national taxpayer advocate appoints local taxpayer advocates (at least one local advocate in each state). They report directly to the national taxpayer advocate and receive their employee evaluations from him. In other words, they aren't in the normal chain of command and thus aren't subject to supervision by and possible interference from local and regional IRS officials.

Taxpayer advocates can issue Taxpayer Assistance Orders (TAOs) when normal IRS procedures impose hardships on taxpayers. For example, a TAO may be issued if questions regarding payment on a taxpayer's account can't be resolved within 30 days or if the IRS poses an immediate threat to seize property. When a TAO is issued, the IRS must halt potentially harmful actions (such as collections) and/or immediately resolve issues at hand (such as properly crediting the taxpayer's account for payments the taxpayer can prove he or she made).

Contact your local IRS office to find out how to get in touch with the taxpayer advocate in your area, or call the National Taxpayer Advocate help line at (877) 777-4778.

**If you win in a tax dispute** with the government, you now can send a bill to the feds for your legal fees (up to $125 per hour, adjusted for inflation) unless the IRS can prove its actions were justified. You may even qualify for reimbursement if you lose in court but made a pretrial offer to the IRS to settle for more than the court-determined amount.

**If the agency acts recklessly** or intentionally disregards the law in an attempt to collect taxes you allegedly owe, you can sue for up to $1 million in civil damages. If the agency acts negligently (a lesser infraction than reckless or intentional disregard of the law), you can sue for civil damages up to $100,000.

**You can recover** up to $1,000 if the agency fails to release a wrongful lien on your property. The IRS must also publish the fact that the lien was wrongful.

**If you are assessed additional taxes,** you will have 10 business days to pay without being charged additional interest, or 21 calendar days for amounts less than $100,000.

**If you enter into an agreement** to fork over underpaid taxes in installments, the IRS must generally give you 30 days' notice of its intent to terminate or modify the deal.

**If you try to settle a tax underpayment** for less than the full amount the IRS wants (a so-called offer in compromise), the local IRS office can now approve discounts of up to $50,000 without clearance from the national office in Washington.

**For payroll taxes,** the feds now can waive late-payment penalties if you're a first-time depositor and you pay up during the first quarter when those taxes are actually due.

**If your refund is disallowed,** the IRS must give you an explanation of the reasons. Previously, the agency wasn't required to provide any explanation.

**If you are hit with interest on back taxes,** there are limits. The government must generally notify you about any alleged problems with your return within 18 months of the filing date. Otherwise, most penalty and interest charges stop accruing after the 18-month period ends. Previously, the IRS could wait up to three years to challenge your return and assess cumulative interest back to Day 1. This provision applies only to individuals and only to income taxes (not estate or gift taxes, employment taxes, etc.). Also, the new rule doesn't apply to the .5% per month penalty on tax underpayments, the 5% per month failure-to-file penalty, or to interest and penalties for fraud and criminal conduct. And your return must be filed on time. The suspension period ends 21 days after the IRS provides a notice that specifically states the amount you owe and the basis for the number.

**If you have both underpayments and overpayments,** the interest rates on each are equalized for noncorporate taxpayers.

**You can confess your tax sins** (within limits) to your CPA or Enrolled Agent, and he can't be forced to testify against you. This so-called accountant-client privilege is similar to the attorney-client privilege that lawyers have long enjoyed. However, as explained on page 53, accountant-client privilege doesn't apply in criminal cases or situations involving corporate tax shelter advice.

**Penalty notices** must state the type of penalty, refer to the tax code section that authorizes the penalty and show how the IRS computed the penalty amount.

**If you go to court** to resolve your tax conflict, the IRS now has the burden of proving you are wrong on factual questions. However, you must have complied with applicable substantiation and recordkeeping requirements and cooperated with the IRS along the road to your court battle. Unfortunately, you still have the burden of proof in dealings outside court, such as when you're negotiating with the IRS Appeals Division.

**You don't need an attorney** to go to Tax Court if the disputed amount is less than $50,000. Previously, the limit for this so-called small-case exception was $10,000.

**The IRS generally can't contact third parties** when investigating your tax situation unless you are notified in advance.

**Seizures of property and liens and levies** now generally require supervisory approval. Previously, revenue agents didn't need any such approval. In addition, the IRS can't seize homes and businesses to satisfy tax liabilities of $5,000 or less. Finally, taxpayers are entitled to a hearing before a lien is levied against their property. Notice of the hearing right must be given at least 30 days before the levy. The notice must also indicate the amount owed, the availability of appeals procedures, how to obtain a release of the lien and the taxpayer's rights with respect to all actions the IRS proposes to take, including any available alternatives to a levy.

**The IRS no longer can issue** retroactive rules via regulations or other guidance (however, rules issued within 18 months of legislation can be retroactive).

## Liberalized Innocent-Spouse Rules

Both spouses (or former spouses) are jointly and severally liable for taxes from years for which they filed joint returns. In other words, the IRS can legally go after either spouse for 100% of any tax shortfall, even if one spouse had nothing to do with the cause of the deficiency and knew nothing about it. Before the 1998 IRS Reform Act, there was a limited exception for "innocent spouses." However, this apparent relief was often not available because of the statutory language and the IRS' insistence on an exceedingly strict interpretation of that language.

Now, taxpayers have three separate avenues for seeking relief from the joint and several liability rule (only one of which is now technically referred to as innocent-spouse relief). Form 8857 (Request for Innocent Spouse Relief) is used to apply for all three. You must file the form within two years of the start of IRS collection activity. The three avenues for taxpayers seeking relief are discussed below.

### *Allocation of tax liabilities*

Joint filers who are divorced or legally separated or have lived apart for the preceding 12 months can elect to compute their separate tax liabilities (based on their share of the couple's income and deductions for the year in question). They are then responsible only for underpayments attributable to their share. However, this relief isn't available if the person seeking relief had actual knowledge of tax underpayments caused by the other party.

### *Innocent spouses*

Innocent-spouse relief is potentially available to all joint filers, including someone still married to the individual with whom he/she filed a joint return. The innocent spouse must show that: (1) she did not know of the understatement, (2) she had no reason to know of the understatement, and (3) it would be unfair to hold her responsible for the understatement after considering all the facts and circumstances. If the person seeking relief knew there were some tax problems but not their full extent, she can still get off the hook for the unknown part.

➤ **Observation:** Innocent-spouse status might be tougher to qualify for than it first appears. Basically, the person seeking relief must be in the dark about the tax problem or at least the full extent of the problem in order to pass the did-not-know part of the test. And she can't simply plead ignorance without failing the did-not-have-any-reason-to-know part of the test. Thus the individual must be both innocent and not ignorant of the problem.

## *Equitable relief*

If the person seeking relief doesn't qualify for allocation of tax liabilities or for innocent-spouse relief, he or she can still be let off the hook if all the facts and circumstances indicate it's unfair to enforce the joint and several liability rule.

*Note:* IRS Publication 1, *Your Rights As a Taxpayer*, summarizes what taxpayers have going for them in the wake of all the recent "taxpayer rights" legislation. To access the publication, go to **www.irs.gov/pub/irs-pdf/p1.pdf**.

# Handling a Correspondence Audit     5

Because this type of audit involves simply an exchange of correspondence, you may believe you can take care of it yourself. It would be wise, however, to consult your accountant or other professional advisor. Show that person the IRS request for certain information, and let the advisor determine whether you can handle the mail audit on your own. In most cases you can, and will, save money by doing so.

For example, if the IRS questions a deduction, you may be able to resolve the query simply by forwarding check receipts to the agency. Why pay for an advisor to do the mailing?

➤ **Observation:** Whether you need an advisor to resolve a correspondence audit really depends on how complicated the IRS request is.

*Rule of Combat No. 8:* When you respond to the IRS, it's a good idea to send a copy of your audit letter along with copies of your documentation. That way, your documents can be filed correctly and forwarded to the right IRS staffers. In too many instances the IRS has said it simply received an envelope crammed with documents without any sort of reference as to why the taxpayer was sending them. It's also wise to send your material by certified mail "return receipt requested" as proof that you responded by the deadline.

If it turns out that the IRS is right and you did forget to report an income item or overstated a deduction, it will generally assess the tax originally owed plus penalty interest dating from the time the tax was due.

## Negligence Penalty

You may also be hit with a 20% negligence penalty based on the tax underpayment. What are your options?

The easiest course is to pay what the agency asks. But you should definitely request a waiver of the negligence penalty if you believe you had a good reason for making the mistake. (Back taxes and interest can't be waived, but the IRS has the discretion to waive the penalty, as it often does with any kind of decent explanation from the taxpayer.)

Although the process is handled through correspondence, all your standard taxpayer's rights apply. Furthermore, if you don't like the way the audit turns out and you believe the IRS is wrong, you can appeal its assessment.

*Rule of Combat No. 9:* Respond to a mail audit promptly. That's key to resolving the issues. Although the IRS may give you 30 days to answer its query, make every effort to respond within 10 days. This will indicate that you're cooperating with the agency and not ignoring the letter.

What are the advantages of a correspondence audit? It saves the taxpayer time, and it doesn't give the IRS auditor an opportunity to ask any further questions. The only way the auditor can obtain more data is to send you a letter asking for additional documentation. Because you don't come face to face with IRS staff, you avoid the possibility of giving embarrassing answers or even volunteering information that might invite further exploration of your return.

## Example of Correspondence Audit and Resolution

A correspondence audit will resemble the real-life example shown on the following pages. It illustrates the type of case a taxpayer should be able to handle without any professional assistance.

If the IRS contacted you for apparently failing to include income reported on an information return, the IRS' letter will show a recomputation of your tax liability and usually assessments of interest and penalties.

On pages 32 and 33 we show the taxpayer's written response to the audit letter and a sample closing letter from the IRS indicating successful resolution of the matter.

# Sample Correspondence Audit

Department of the Treasury
**Internal Revenue Service**
Austin, TX 78767

Notice No.: xxxxx
Notice Date: 9/09/06
Social Security No.: xxx-xx-xxxx
Form: 1040     Tax Year: 2004

THIS NOTICE REQUIRES A RESPONSE.
Please complete the response page at the end of this notice and send it to us in the enclosed envelope.

Joe Taxpayer
Address
City, State, ZIP

For additional information, please phone TeleTax 1-800-829-4477 (toll free) and request Topic Number 652. Where you may call us: 1-800-829-1040

### WE ARE PROPOSING CHANGES TO YOUR 2004 TAX RETURN

We are proposing changes to your 2004 income tax return because information you reported does not match what was reported to us by your employers, banks, and/or other payers. Our proposed amount you owe is $25,533.00. See our proposed changes on page 2 and the detailed information beginning on page 3.

Please compare your records with the payer information. It shows the information we used for our proposed changes. To assist you in reviewing your return, the payer information may show both reported and unreported amounts. However, the proposed changes shown on page 2 are based on the unreported amounts only.

| If You AGREE with our Proposed Changes: | If You DISAGREE with our Proposed Changes: |
|---|---|
| *Check Box A on the response page at the end of this notice. | *Check Box B on the response page at the end of this notice. |
| *Sign and date the total agreement statement, and | *Enclose a signed statement explaining each change you disagree with and why you disagree. |
| *Send us the response page in the enclosed envelope. | *Include any supporting documents you wish us to consider, and |
| *If possible, enclose your payment in full. If you cannot pay the entire amount, you can request an installment agreement by completing the last page of this notice. | *Send us the response page with your statement and supporting documents in the enclosed envelope. |

It is important that we receive your response by 10/09/06. If we do not receive your response, we will conclude that our proposed changes are correct. Then we will send you a Notice of Deficiency followed by a bill for the proposed amount you owe, including tax and any penalties plus additional interest.

*(continued on page 30)*

## Our Proposed Changes to Your 2004 Form 1040
### (Detailed Information for These Changes Begins on Page 3)

|  | Shown on Return | Reported to IRS (or Proposed by IRS) | Proposed Change |
|---|---|---|---|
| Our Proposed Changes to Your Income and Deductions |  |  |  |
| IRA Distribution | $0.00 | $38,980.00 | $38,980.00 |
| Schedule A Itemized Deductions | $371.00 | $1,541.00 | $1,170.00 |
| Schedule A Limitation (Itemized Deductions Worksheet, Line 9) |  |  |  |
| Total Increase |  |  | $40,150.00 |

Our Proposed Changes to Your Tax Computation

| | | | |
|---|---|---|---|
| 1. Exemption Amount, line 36 | $ 6,885.00 | $ 4,437.00 | $–2,448.00 |
| 2. Taxable Income, line 37 | $112,601.00 | $155,199.00 | $42,598.00 |
| 3. Tax, line 38 | $ 30,042.00 | $ 44,942.00 | $14,900.00 |
| 4. Self-Employment Tax, line 45 | $ 11,429.00 | $ 11,429.00 | $ 0.00 |
| 5. Other Taxes, lines 46–50 | $ 0.00 | $ 3,898.00 | $ 3,898.00 |
| 6. Total Taxes, line 51 | $ 41,471.00 | $ 60,269.00 | $18,798.00 |
| 7. Net Tax Increase | | | $18,798.00 |
| 8. Accuracy-Related Penalty | | | $ 3,760.00 |
| 9. Interest From 4/15/2005 to 09/24/2006 | | | $ 2,975.00 |
| 10. Proposed Amount You Owe IRS | | | $25,533.00 |

(The proposed changes apply to this notice only. It doesn't include any additional amounts for tax year 2004 that you may owe from a previous IRS notice.)

### Explanation of Changes

Rollover of IRA or Lump-Sum Distribution
If you rolled over your IRA or lump-sum distribution, please send us a statement from the payer with:
—The amount of your rollover,
—The date of your rollover, and
—The date of your distribution.

Premature Distributions Tax From a Qualified Retirement Plan
Our proposed increase to your tax includes an additional tax on a premature distribution from your qualified retirement plan. The tax is 10% of the taxable part of your premature distribution and is included in the tax computation on page 2.

The 10% tax does not apply if the distribution was rolled over to another qualified retirement plan within 60 days or if you were disabled or at least 59½ years old at the time of the distribution.

If you rolled your distribution over to another plan within 60 days, please send us a statement showing:
—The amount you rolled over,
—The date you received the distribution,

—The date the funds were deposited in another retirement plan, and
—The name of the retirement plan that received the funds.

If the distribution was exempt from the 10% tax because you were disabled or at least 59½ years old, please send us a statement showing the reason for the exemption. Other exceptions may apply as indicated in Publication 17, Your Federal Income Tax, or Publication 590, Individual Retirement Arrangements.

LIMIT ON SCHEDULE A ITEMIZED DEDUCTIONS
We limited the amount of Schedule A Itemized Deductions you may claim because your adjusted gross income is more than $128,950.

EXEMPTIONS DEDUCTION REDUCED (FOR SINGLE TAXPAYERS)
We reduced your exemptions deduction because your adjusted gross income is more than $128,950. At this amount, the deduction begins to be reduced or eliminated for taxpayers whose tax year 2004 filing status is SINGLE.

ACCURACY-RELATED PENALTY DUE TO SUBSTANTIAL UNDERSTATEMENT OF TAX
Since the proposed increase in your tax is more than the greater of $5,000 or 10% of your corrected tax, the law requires us to charge a penalty for substantial understatement of tax. This penalty is 20% of your proposed increase in tax. We may reduce the penalty if you have substantial authority for any of the underclaimed income or overclaimed deductions shown on this notice.

If you have a reason why we should reduce or waive this penalty, please write to us and:
—Tell us the substantial authority (Internal Revenue Code, Regulations, Revenue
    Rulings, etc.) you used to determine how to treat your income, and
—Tell us where on your return you clearly show the facts that support your
    treatment of the income.

We will review your information and determine if we should reduce the penalty.

INTEREST PERIOD
Generally, we figure interest on the proposed tax change in this notice from the due date of your return, April 15, 2005, to 15 days after the date of this notice. If we receive your full payment by then, interest stops. If we do not, interest continues until you pay your balance in full. If you received a refund(s) without interest for 2004 that was less than the proposed tax change in this notice:
—We figured interest from the date your refund(s) was issued to 15 days after
    the date of this notice on that portion of the proposed tax change that
    matches your refund(s).
—We then figured interest from the due date of your return to 15 days after the
    date of this notice on that portion of the proposed tax change that exceeds
    your refund(s).

If you received a refund(s) without interest for 2004 that was equal to or greater than the proposed tax change in this notice, we figured interest from the date your refund(s) was issued to 15 days after the date of this notice.

We do not charge interest prior to the due date of the return regardless of when you received your refund(s).

*(continued on page 32)*

MISIDENTIFIED INCOME
If any of the income shown on this notice is not yours, send us the name, address, and social security number of the person who received the income. Please notify the payers to correct their records to show the name and social security number of the person who actually received the income so that future reports to us are accurate.

---

Your payers reported the following information to us:

[Name of Bank]        ISSUED FORM 1099-R TO SS NO.: xxx-xx-xxxx
                      GROSS DISTRIBUTION              $38,980
                      TAXABLE AMOUNT                  $38,980

ACCOUNT NO.: xxxxx

If you agree with our proposed changes, please do not file an amended 2004 federal tax return (Form 1040X). However, you may need to file an amended state income tax return. We send information to your state and local tax agencies about any change in your income tax as a result of this notice. If our proposed changes affect your state income tax, file an amended state income tax return as soon as possible.

Please review your records and returns filed after 2004 to make sure all income was reported correctly. If income was not reported correctly, you should file an amended federal and state income tax return for each year and pay any tax and interest you owe as soon as possible to avoid additional interest and penalties.

---

*[The following letter was the taxpayer's response to the IRS' proposed changes to his 2004 tax return.]*

MEMO TO:   WHOM IT MAY CONCERN
FROM:      JOE TAXPAYER
RE:        SS NO.: xxx-xx-xxxx
           NOTICE NO.: xxxxxx
           FORM/YEAR: 1040 FOR 2004
DATE:      9/24/06

Dear Sir or Madam:

Regarding the proposed changes to my 2004 tax return . . . I disagree with all of the proposed changes, which relate to a 2004 IRA distribution in the amount of $38,980.54. The distribution occurred on 12/10/04, as shown on the enclosed summary statement from the IRA trustee [a large bank]. The distribution was rolled over into another IRA on 1/21/05, as shown on the enclosed statement from the trustee for the rollover IRA [a large brokerage house]. Since the rollover occurred within 60 days of the distribution, the distribution was nontaxable. Accordingly, all of the proposed changes do not apply.

In preparing my Form 1040, I should have reported $38,981 on Line 15a and zero on Line 15b. Instead, I simply left both lines blank. In any case, the correct taxable amount was zero, as indicated on the return.

Thank you in advance for promptly resolving this matter and removing the proposed assessments of additional tax, penalties, and interest from my account.

If you have any questions, please feel free to contact me at [phone number] between 9 a.m. and 5 p.m. on weekdays.

Very truly yours,
[signature]
JOE TAXPAYER


*[Here's how the IRS replied to the taxpayer's letter.]*

| Department of the Treasury | Notice No.: | xxxxx |
|---|---|---|
| **Internal Revenue Service** | Notice Date: | 9/09/06 |
| Austin, TX 78767 | Social Security No.: | xxx-xx-xxxx |
| | Form: 1040 | Tax Year: 2004 |

| Joe Taxpayer | For Assistance, You May Call: |
|---|---|
| Address | Person to Call: xxxxxxx |
| City, State, ZIP | Number to Call: xxxxxx |

## Closing Letter

Thank you for giving us more information about the income we recently wrote to you about. We are pleased to tell you that, with your help, we were able to clear up the differences between your records and your payers' records. If you sent us a payment based on our proposed changes, we will refund it to you if you owe no other taxes or have no other debts the law requires us to collect.

If you have already received a notice of deficiency, you may disregard it. You won't need to file a petition with the United States Tax Court to reconsider the tax you owe. If you have already filed a petition, the office of the District Counsel will contact you on the final closing of this case.

If you have questions about this notice, please write to us at the address shown above. Include your telephone number and the best time for us to call you if we need more information. If you prefer, you may call the person whose name and telephone number are listed above. Since that number may be long-distance for you, you may want to call the number listed for the IRS in your local directory instead. Employees there may be able to help you, but the office at the address shown on this notice is most familiar with your case.

Thank you for your cooperation.

# Meeting the IRS Face to Face      6

Until now, you as a taxpayer have been forced to deal with the IRS through the mail or, at worst, on the telephone. But it's another matter when you receive a contact letter that sets an appointed time for you to face an IRS auditor. You have a big choice to make: Do you go in person, or do you send someone you have empowered to represent you?

In either case, you'll have to assemble the requested documents. As indicated earlier, the contact letter usually includes a checklist of items the auditor wants to see. Generally, this means the audit will be limited to two or three items. However, remember: Your entire tax return is subject to examination if the auditor becomes interested in other issues. In that case, the auditor would have to obtain permission from her supervisor before she could raise new issues.

With the contact letter, the IRS encloses information guides to assist you in selecting the types of documents required to substantiate the two to three items the agency is questioning. For examples of the specific information needed to substantiate various items, see page 39.

## The IRS Is Prepared—Are You?

Before you make any decision about who should meet with the IRS, you should know how "well armed" the IRS auditor is. If it's an individual return, chances are that the auditor won't be totally familiar with it until you or your representative walks into the IRS office on the date of the audit. The auditor will take merely a few minutes to become acquainted with the return and the issues in question. Nevertheless, you're somewhat at a disadvantage because the burden of proof rests with you.

Also keep in mind that the auditor has a psychological edge by conducting examinations day in, day out. For you, the audit is a new and possibly intimidating experience—not to mention your fear of the prospect of paying more taxes, interest charges and perhaps penalty fees to boot. Moreover, be aware that the odds of leaving an office audit without owing at least some additional tax are *against* you, regardless of whether you go in person or send a representative. As IRS records indicate, once a return has run the gauntlet of the computerized DIF scoring system and later employee screening, there's about a 75% chance the owner of that return will leave an office audit owing additional tax. But if you're really lucky, your return may be among the approximately 5% that end up with a refund after an office examination.

### *Battle of the bulge*

If the tax return involves a business, the auditor's file may be an inch thick even before the audit request letter is sent. In other words, the auditor has spent a good deal of time scrutinizing a business return. Long before a business taxpayer is summoned for a field examination, the auditor has at least done the following:

- **Looked over all the documents** in the taxpayer's file. This may include an Information Returns Program Report, which contains data on wages, dividends, interest and other forms of income received by the taxpayer. The file may also contain a Currency Transaction Report for cash transactions of $10,000 or more, or even an informant's report from a disgruntled employee who may have noticed the taxpayer violating tax procedures.
- **Reviewed the results of any prior audits.** If you're a business taxpayer and have faced an office audit, the agent may ask you whether your business had ever been audited in the past. Let's hope you didn't lie because the auditor asking that question already knows the answer. He probably was just trying to find out at the outset how honest you were.
- **Pored over your return** for any unusual items that could be sticking points. At the auditor's disposal is the taxpayer's income tax return balance sheet (unless the business is a sole proprietorship), which can be very revealing to the IRS.

## Should You Send a Representative?

Obviously, it depends on how confident you are of both your records and ability to perform competently as your own advocate. Keep in mind that you can solicit assistance from your attorney or accountant without actually having to pay him or her to represent you formally at meetings with the auditor. For example, you can have your accountant review the documents you're taking to the examination. Or you can have your attorney look them over to make sure they respond to the issues the IRS has pointed out.

➤ **Observation:** An important reason for having someone familiar with the audit process represent you before the IRS is simple: Being inexperienced in the process, you might blurt out more information than you should, or even lose your cool with the examiner. In one case, for example, a doctor lost his temper when the auditor disallowed a small item. In his anger, the doctor snapped that he couldn't justify another deduction he took that wasn't even under consideration in the audit. The auditor ended up disallowing that one, too, which added $2,300 to the doctor's bill. A seasoned tax advisor wouldn't rise to that kind of bait. Rather, he would try to minimize any damage while looking for ways to make up for it elsewhere in the return.

However, unless it's difficult for you to make the meeting or you feel out of your depth talking about tax matters, it may not be necessary to have someone represent you during an office examination. After all, it's your return, your income and your deductions under scrutiny. In many instances, a representative might eventually have to come to you anyway for the answers the IRS is seeking.

In any case, it's up to you to assemble the documentation—and if you have it, you're basically home free. Although taxpayers find it hard to believe, the IRS auditor is supposed to be strictly neutral and interested solely in determining the correct tax. The auditor will be swayed by good records, not by the glibness of an "expert."

If you decide to go it alone and then run into a thorny problem, you're always within your rights to suspend the interview and consult with your attorney or accountant. At that point, you also can punt if necessary and formally engage the accountant or attorney to represent you the rest of the way. **Bottom line:** You often can save money by answering the call of the IRS yourself.

Reminder: If you decide to engage a representative to handle the whole matter, you must fill out Form 2848 (Power of Attorney and Declaration of Representative), shown on page 43.

## Deciding to Go It Alone

Let's suppose you've decided to deal with the problem on your own. You don't have to show up on the day the IRS has assigned to you in the contact letter. You can get an extension by calling the phone number on your appointment letter. Just give the clerk a reasonable excuse, such as the fact you have a business appointment on the day the IRS asked you to come in. Or, tell the IRS you need more time to secure the necessary records.

That first extension is almost automatic. And you probably can get a second extension if you have a plausible excuse. After that, though, you risk planting the seed of suspicion that you're requesting extensions because you really have something to hide.

If you decide not to show up at all for the office examination, you lose—or at least that's how the IRS sees it. The agency simply will disallow any questionable items that you've claimed on your return. Officially, you get a "30-day letter," which states that you have 30 days to tell the auditor whether you agree or disagree with the findings and whether you intend to appeal. You may request an appeal within the IRS. If you don't pursue an appeal, or if your appeal is unsuccessful, you will receive a Notice of Deficiency, or "90-Day Letter" (*see page 65*). This letter states you have 90 days to file a petition with the U.S. Tax Court or you will receive a bill for the tax you owe.

***Rule of Combat No. 10:*** *Sometimes, it may pay to ignore the notice for an office audit if the issues questioned by the IRS fall into a gray area that might be hard to prove, and if those same issues are present in your past returns as well as the return for the year under audit. By ignoring the IRS request for an office examination, you tacitly agree to pay the additional tax on those items, but only for the tax year being questioned. Then it becomes a closed matter. By not showing up for the audit, you cut the chances of other, prior returns being checked for those gray-area claims.*

## Dredging Up Those Old Returns and Documents

If you can't find your copy of an old tax return that the IRS might be questioning, you have several moves to try. If you paid someone to prepare your return, it should be readily available from him; many preparers keep copies for several years.

When you need only certain information and not the return itself, you can obtain the facts fairly quickly by contacting your local IRS office and filling out

Form 4506 (Request for Copy or Transcript of Tax Form). You'll receive a sheet showing your name and Social Security number, the type of return you filed (1040, 1040A, 1040EZ), tax shown on the return, adjusted gross income, taxable income, self-employment tax and the number of exemptions you claimed. There is no charge to obtain this.

If you need an actual copy of the return, however, you will have to check a different box on Form 4506, pay a nominal fee for each year's return you need and wait five weeks or so.

In addition to copies of your tax schedules and statements, you should assemble receipts, bills, invoices, canceled checks and other documents needed to resolve the IRS issues. If your deductions are being questioned, for example, now is the time—before the actual examination—to ensure that your receipts add up to the figure you inserted on Schedule A. The auditor is going to ask you how you arrived at the figure on your tax form. You'll want to present the auditor with the receipts or bills that total up to the amount of the deduction you took.

## How to Reconstruct Your Records—Legally

In the less-than-perfect world we live in, chances are that you may not be able to produce receipts, bills or other written documentation for all the items on your return that are at issue (especially when the audit arises several years after the end of the tax year in question). That's when you must turn to reconstructing your records or amassing the best proof you have for the IRS.

It's perfectly legal to reconstruct your records in any way to provide adequate evidence that what you claimed on your return was, in fact, correct. The law doesn't require perfect recordkeeping habits—it's just simpler that way.

For interest payments, medical expenses and so forth, one way to reconstruct records is to secure a statement or affidavit from the parties involved. Or, you may be able to prove up expenses by reviewing your credit card statements even though the receipts are missing. In the case of contributions of more than $250 to charitable organizations, however, you are required by law to have obtained a receipt by the time you filed the return claiming the deduction. Contrary to what some think, this rule doesn't throw you out if you lost the receipt. You have to prove only that you *had* it at the time. A statement from the charity or a photocopy of the receipt from its records is sufficient.

If you received or paid interest, obtain a statement from the second party. With a contribution of clothing to a charity, you might prove the value by itemizing the articles donated, their dates of purchase and the prices you paid. Try to show the IRS examiner a pattern of clothing purchases you have for keeping up with style and the stores where you buy clothing to indicate the level of prices you normally pay.

When statements from involved parties are lacking, try to amass facts that will prove a deduction. You may have a day planner that indicates you attended a seminar or event in which travel expenses were incurred. In the case of a casualty loss, for example, you might secure a copy of a police report to prove to the IRS examiner that the loss did, in fact, take place.

The auditor probably will give you the benefit of the doubt if your secondary proof is orderly and represents your honest intentions.

## Table 4: Documents Needed to Verify Audit Items

| Item | Proof |
|---|---|
| **Exemptions (children)** | Birth certificates. |
| | If divorced, submit divorce decree and Form 8332 indicating which parent will claim the exemption. |
| | Canceled checks and receipts for amounts you spent on support of children. |
| | Records of what others spent on the children, including amounts received from Social Security, welfare and other outside sources. |
| | A Social Security number must be obtained for each child and reported on your return. |
| **Exemptions (other than your children)** | A dollar listing of the cost of the dependent's support. |
| | The amount of income received by or for the dependent. |
| | A compilation of what each member of the household spent toward household expenses. |
| | Name, address and Social Security number of persons with whom dependent lived during the tax year. |
| | Copies of canceled checks and receipts to verify amounts spent for the dependent. |
| | A Social Security number must be reported for each person claimed as an exemption on your return. |
| **Medical expenses** | Canceled checks and receipts for all medical and dental expenses. |
| | Itemized receipts for drugs and medicines. |
| **Medical travel** | A physician's statement showing the days on which you had an appointment. |
| | Receipts for parking and tolls. |
| | Taxicab receipts or a log showing number of miles you traveled for medical reasons. |
| **Medical insurance premiums** | Your insurance policy, along with canceled checks/receipts indicating premium payments. |

| | |
|---|---|
| **Taxes** | Canceled checks or receipts for taxes you paid. In the case of state and city taxes, furnish copies of prior year's state or city tax return, along with canceled checks showing payment. |
| **Interest** | Canceled checks, along with receipts or statements from creditors indicating amounts of interest you paid. For mortgage interest, present year-end statements. |
| **Investment expenses** | Canceled checks and receipts. |
| **Sales of stocks/securities** | Copies of brokerage firm's confirmation slips that show buy and sell prices. |
| **Contributions** | Canceled checks, receipts or a statement from a religious organization or other non-profit group. (A canceled check is no longer sufficient for contributions of $250 or more.) |
| | For donation of property, show a receipt from donee, a list of items contributed and fair market value of items at time of contribution. For large contributions, a professional appraisal is required *(see Form 8283)*. |
| **Casualty losses** | Damage reports from police or fire department. |
| | Receipts or canceled checks indicating the basis of the involved property and the date you acquired it. |
| | Documents showing fair market value of property before and after the casualty. |
| | Records of appraisals or damage estimates. |
| | Repair bills or estimates of repairs. |
| | Insurance reports on reimbursement amounts. |
| | Photographs, if available, indicating the extent of loss or damage. |
| **Child care** | Canceled checks or receipts, along with the name, address and Social Security number of the individual caring for your child. |
| **Alimony** | Canceled checks showing payment. |
| | A copy of the divorce or separate-maintenance agreement. |
| | Current address of former spouse and his or her Social Security number. |

| | |
|---|---|
| **Reimbursed education expenses** | Canceled checks and receipts for tuition and for other pertinent expenses, such as books, meals, lodging. |
| | A report from your employer on reimbursement it provided, along with a statement of the purpose of your study and that it was required for your job or otherwise qualified as a tax-free reimbursement. |
| | School transcript showing courses taken and when. |
| **Bad debts** | Name and address of debtor. |
| | Promissory notes or other written documentation of legal debt. Proof of the improbability of collecting the funds. |
| **Travel & entertainment expenses** | *For business travel:* Canceled checks and receipts for gas, oil, auto insurance and lease payments; auto repair bills; invoice for business auto; log or diary showing business miles driven. |
| | *For entertainment:* (1) Receipts and canceled checks indicating date, amount, place, person entertained and the business purpose for the activity. (2) A statement from your employer that shows the amount of reimbursement and says you were required to incur such expenses. |
| **Home office expenses** | Receipts or canceled checks for mortgage interest, taxes, rent, utilities, office repairs, furniture and equipment. |
| | A statement from your employer that it requires you to work out of your home for its convenience, and that it doesn't provide you with an office. |
| | Photos of your office area (it need not be a separate room). Keep in mind that no personal activity can take place in space set aside for business unless it's used for inventory storage or is a day care business. |
| **Rental income & expenses** | *For proof of income:* (1) Receipts for rents, deposits and fees. (2) A list of your tenants, their monthly rents and the months of occupancy. |

*For expenses:* (1) Canceled checks, invoices for repairs and costs associated with rental units, such as gardening. (2) Year-end mortgage statement, plus canceled checks for payment of interest and taxes. (3) To prove depreciation, documents showing original cost, tax bill for year property was purchased, plus rental record for the year prior to the tax year the auditor is examining.

**Business income & expenses**

These are Schedule C items.

*For proof of income:* All available records, such as bank statements, cash-receipts journals, invoices and Forms 1099. Also included are records of loans and receipts indicating repayment, and statements for sales of real estate or property.

*For expenses:* Ledgers and journals, invoices, payroll tax returns, and canceled checks and receipts.

**IRA rollovers**

Trustee forms and account statements showing that withdrawn funds or securities were rolled over tax-free within 60 days of withdrawal.

**Penalty-free IRA withdrawals**

Receipts or canceled checks showing qualified expenditures for higher education expenses, certain home purchase costs, etc.

**Dependent child tax credit**

Same as for dependent exemption.

**Education tax credits**

Receipts or canceled checks showing qualified tuition and fee expenditures. For Hope Scholarship credit, report cards showing student carried at least half a full-time load for at least one academic term during the year.

**College loan interest**

Receipts or canceled checks showing payment of qualified tuition and/or room and board expenses within a reasonable time before or after the loan is taken out.

**Depreciation of "listed property"**

For autos; computers and peripheral equipment; video, audio, photographic equipment; and cellular phones: usage logs or other documentation showing business and personal use.

# Form 2848
(Rev. July 2014)
Department of the Treasury
Internal Revenue Service

# Power of Attorney
# and Declaration of Representative

▶ Information about Form 2848 and its instructions is at *www.irs.gov/form2848*.

OMB No. 1545-0150

**For IRS Use Only**
Received by:
Name _____
Telephone _____
Function _____
Date / /

## Part I  Power of Attorney

**Caution:** *A separate Form 2848 must be completed for each taxpayer. Form 2848 will not be honored for any purpose other than representation before the IRS.*

**1  Taxpayer information.** Taxpayer must sign and date this form on page 2, line 7.

| Taxpayer name and address | Taxpayer identification number(s) |
|---|---|
|  | Daytime telephone number | Plan number (if applicable) |

hereby appoints the following representative(s) as attorney(s)-in-fact:

**2  Representative(s)** must sign and date this form on page 2, Part II.

Name and address
CAF No. _____
PTIN _____
Telephone No. _____
Fax No. _____
**Check if to be sent copies of notices and communications** ☐    Check if new: Address ☐    Telephone No. ☐    Fax No. ☐

Name and address
CAF No. _____
PTIN _____
Telephone No. _____
Fax No. _____
**Check if to be sent copies of notices and communications** ☐    Check if new: Address ☐    Telephone No. ☐    Fax No. ☐

Name and address
CAF No. _____
PTIN _____
Telephone No. _____
Fax No. _____
**(Note.** IRS sends notices and communications to only two representatives.)    Check if new: Address ☐    Telephone No. ☐    Fax No. ☐

Name and address
CAF No. _____
PTIN _____
Telephone No. _____
Fax No. _____
**(Note.** IRS sends notices and communications to only two representatives.)    Check if new: Address ☐    Telephone No. ☐    Fax No. ☐

to represent the taxpayer before the Internal Revenue Service and perform the following acts:

**3  Acts authorized (you are required to complete this line 3).** With the exception of the acts described in line 5b, I authorize my representative(s) to receive and inspect my confidential tax information and to perform acts that I can perform with respect to the tax matters described below. For example, my representative(s) shall have the authority to sign any agreements, consents, or similar documents (see instructions for line 5a for authorizing a representative to sign a return).

| Description of Matter (Income, Employment, Payroll, Excise, Estate, Gift, Whistleblower, Practitioner Discipline, PLR, FOIA, Civil Penalty, Sec. 5000A Shared Responsibility Payment, Sec. 4980H Shared Responsibility Payment, etc.) (see instructions) | Tax Form Number (1040, 941, 720, etc.) (if applicable) | Year(s) or Period(s) (if applicable) (see instructions) |
|---|---|---|
|  |  |  |
|  |  |  |
|  |  |  |

**4  Specific use not recorded on Centralized Authorization File (CAF).** If the power of attorney is for a specific use not recorded on CAF, check this box. See the instructions for **Line 4. Specific Use Not Recorded on CAF** . . . . . . . . . . . . . . . . . ▶ ☐

**5a  Additional acts authorized.** In addition to the acts listed on line 3 above, I authorize my representative(s) to perform the following acts (see instructions for line 5a for more information):

☐ Authorize disclosure to third parties;     ☐ Substitute or add representative(s);     ☐ Sign a return; _____

_____

☐ Other acts authorized: _____

_____

For Privacy Act and Paperwork Reduction Act Notice, see the instructions.         Cat. No. 11980J         Form **2848** (Rev. 7-2014)

Form 2848 (Rev. 7-2014) Page **2**

**b  Specific acts not authorized.** My representative(s) is (are) not authorized to endorse or otherwise negotiate any check (including directing or accepting payment by any means, electronic or otherwise, into an account owned or controlled by the representative(s) or any firm or other entity with whom the representative(s) is (are) associated) issued by the government in respect of a federal tax liability.
List any specific deletions to the acts otherwise authorized in this power of attorney (see instructions for line 5b): _____

**6  Retention/revocation of prior power(s) of attorney.** The filing of this power of attorney automatically revokes all earlier power(s) of attorney on file with the Internal Revenue Service for the same matters and years or periods covered by this document. If you **do not** want to revoke a prior power of attorney, check here  . . . . . . . . . . . . . . . . . . . . . . . . . . ▶ ☐
**YOU MUST ATTACH A COPY OF ANY POWER OF ATTORNEY YOU WANT TO REMAIN IN EFFECT.**

**7  Signature of taxpayer.** If a tax matter concerns a year in which a joint return was filed, each spouse must file a separate power of attorney even if they are appointing the same representative(s). If signed by a corporate officer, partner, guardian, tax matters partner, executor, receiver, administrator, or trustee on behalf of the taxpayer, I certify that I have the authority to execute this form on behalf of the taxpayer.

▶ **IF NOT COMPLETED, SIGNED, AND DATED, THE IRS WILL RETURN THIS POWER OF ATTORNEY TO THE TAXPAYER.**

| Signature | Date | Title (if applicable) |
|---|---|---|
| Print Name | | Print name of taxpayer from line 1 if other than individual |

## Part II  Declaration of Representative

Under penalties of perjury, by my signature below I declare that:
- I am not currently suspended or disbarred from practice before the Internal Revenue Service;
- I am subject to regulations contained in Circular 230 (31 CFR, Subtitle A, Part 10), as amended, governing practice before the Internal Revenue Service;
- I am authorized to represent the taxpayer identified in Part I for the matter(s) specified there; and
- I am one of the following:

  **a** Attorney—a member in good standing of the bar of the highest court of the jurisdiction shown below.
  **b** Certified Public Accountant—duly qualified to practice as a certified public accountant in the jurisdiction shown below.
  **c** Enrolled Agent—enrolled as an agent by the Internal Revenue Service per the requirements of Circular 230.
  **d** Officer—a bona fide officer of the taxpayer organization.
  **e** Full-Time Employee—a full-time employee of the taxpayer.
  **f** Family Member—a member of the taxpayer's immediate family (for example, spouse, parent, child, grandparent, grandchild, step-parent, step-child, brother, or sister).
  **g** Enrolled Actuary—enrolled as an actuary by the Joint Board for the Enrollment of Actuaries under 29 U.S.C. 1242 (the authority to practice before the Internal Revenue Service is limited by section 10.3(d) of Circular 230).
  **h** Unenrolled Return Preparer—Your authority to practice before the Internal Revenue Service is limited. You must have been eligible to sign the return under examination and have prepared and signed the return. **See Notice 2011-6 and *Special rules for registered tax return preparers and unenrolled return preparers* in the instructions (PTIN required for designation h).**
  **i** Registered Tax Return Preparer—registered as a tax return preparer under the requirements of section 10.4 of Circular 230. Your authority to practice before the Internal Revenue Service is limited. You must have been eligible to sign the return under examination and have prepared and signed the return. **See Notice 2011-6 and *Special rules for registered tax return preparers and unenrolled return preparers* in the instructions (PTIN required for designation i).**
  **k** Student Attorney or CPA—receives permission to represent taxpayers before the IRS by virtue of his/her status as a law, business, or accounting student working in an LITC or STCP. See instructions for Part II for additional information and requirements.
  **r** Enrolled Retirement Plan Agent—enrolled as a retirement plan agent under the requirements of Circular 230 (the authority to practice before the Internal Revenue Service is limited by section 10.3(e)).

▶ **IF THIS DECLARATION OF REPRESENTATIVE IS NOT COMPLETED, SIGNED, AND DATED, THE IRS WILL RETURN THE POWER OF ATTORNEY. REPRESENTATIVES MUST SIGN IN THE ORDER LISTED IN PART I, LINE 2.** See the instructions for Part II.

**Note.** For designations d-f, enter your title, position, or relationship to the taxpayer in the "Licensing jurisdiction" column. See the instructions for Part II for more information.

| Designation— Insert above letter **(a–r)** | Licensing jurisdiction (state) or other licensing authority (if applicable) | Bar, license, certification, registration, or enrollment number (if applicable). See instructions for Part II for more information. | Signature | Date |
|---|---|---|---|---|
| | | | | |
| | | | | |
| | | | | |

Form **2848** (Rev. 7-2014)

# Enduring an Office Audit

# 7

Yours is probably one of about five office audits that your particular IRS auditor will conduct in a normal day. Expect to stay about an hour and a half for a regular return. For a Schedule C business return, your stay might last up to four hours.

At this juncture, we should mention another statutory protection that you may want to employ. The law offers taxpayers the right to make a sound recording of any interview with an IRS employee involving the assessment or collection of tax.

You have some procedural hoops to jump through, however. You have to give the IRS 10 days' notice if you want to record the interview. You also must supply your own recording equipment, permit the agency to make its own recording and present yourself at a location (usually an IRS office) where the agency can make its own recording.

If the IRS chooses to record the session, you can obtain a transcript or a copy of its recording if you ask for it within 30 days and are willing to repay the agency's cost of providing it.

## Meeting the IRS Auditor

Make sure you arrive on time, since the auditor's schedule is often fine-tuned. Hand your appointment letter to the clerk. Once you're ushered to the auditor's desk, make sure you follow this checklist:

✔ **Be courteous.** This will set the tone for the examination. You obviously don't want to be hostile or intimidating. Although your documentation will carry the day, first impressions do influence the auditor. Make sure you're polite.

✔ **Come prepared to take notes** if you decide not to record the session. You will have to make a list of any items the auditor may need from you to complete the examination.

✔ **Also make sure** that you have all the documents and written information to support your contentions on the tax points raised by the IRS. Technically, an auditor can go to almost any length to verify the accuracy of a return, but as a general rule, she will rely on your documents. If she needs further information, she'll give you time to supply it.

✔ **Present your documentation** to the auditor one piece at a time, as you're asked. After the auditor has looked at the document, take it back and put it away.

*Rule of Combat No. 11: Don't give the auditor the opportunity to retain a document and possibly find something wrong after further reflection. Make the auditor ask you for the document again if that becomes necessary.*

✔ **Be credible.** Show receipts to prove your point. If you're asked about an item for which you don't have a receipt, tell the auditor you will have to reconstruct the record. IRS rules do allow the auditor to make reasonable allowances, but the auditor will offer them only if she thinks you're credible.

✔ **Don't lie.** That should go without saying. You can receive a hefty fine or even be jailed for not telling the truth.

✔ **Stay cool** when fielding tough questions. For example, if you don't understand why the auditor is asking a certain question, it's perfectly within your rights to ask about it. Most of the time, you'll probably get a suitable answer and then you can reply.

✔ **If the auditor** confronts you with something like "I don't have to tell you why I'm asking the question," simply say you're not sure of the answer and will need more time to respond adequately.

➤ **Recommendation:** If you really don't know the answer, don't try to wing it. Admit you don't know and say you'll find out. And, of course, be sure you do get back to the examiner with the answer.

✔ **If you run** into a belligerent auditor, you can counter by asking for the name and telephone number of her supervisor. If that doesn't work and she continues to be hostile, you're within your rights to report the auditor to a supervisor.

*Rule of Combat No. 12: Keep in mind that if you sense a definite personality clash with the auditor, you can summon his or her supervisor and request that another auditor be assigned to your case. Having said that, it's still best to try hard to get along with the auditor before asking for a replacement.*

✔ **Important:** Answer only the specific questions you're asked. The auditor's main activity during the audit involves scanning and totaling the figures on your return. You may be asked how you arrived at a particular figure.

Don't volunteer extra information. It could raise more questions and prompt the auditor to venture off in new directions that are fraught with peril for you. As we said earlier, the auditor has a fairly simple game plan in the majority of cases. Let her stick to it.

If you decided to represent yourself because the amounts involved in the audit are small, be especially wary if the auditor raises an issue that wasn't mentioned in the original audit letter.

Don't give an off-the-cuff answer, which could needlessly damage your position. It's generally better to say that you'll need time to study your records because the notice didn't mention the subject. That statement allows you time to compose a considered response. Or the auditor may never raise the issue again, and it will go away by itself.

## How Your Audit May End

At the conclusion of your examination, you face four possible outcomes:

**1.** The auditor may propose no change in your tax liability.

**2.** The auditor may propose adjustments to your tax liability, and you agree to those adjustments.

**3.** The auditor may propose adjustments, and you're willing to agree to some, but not all.

**4.** The auditor may propose adjustments, and you're unwilling to agree to any of them.

If you should happen to receive a "no change" decision, thank your lucky stars. The process is almost over. You will receive a follow-up letter stating that the IRS has accepted your return as filed.

Unfortunately, one of the other three outcomes is more likely. In Section 9 we will review the steps you can take in that event. First, however, we'll turn to the third type of examination, the field audit.

# BRACING FOR A FIELD AUDIT      8

Many businesses and some individuals who have large and complex returns have to endure a field audit. The IRS may launch a field audit if it strongly suspects that you failed to report substantial amounts of income. These audits are so named because they take place in "the field," meaning at your place of business or possibly in your home.

To put it bluntly, getting hit with a field audit is the worst-case scenario. The process is cumbersome and usually time-consuming. Auditors generally approach field audits with a heightened sense of skepticism.

Because both office and field audits entail meeting IRS personnel face to face, the procedures for preparing for them are similar. The field audit, however, is more comprehensive because you face a more rigorously trained IRS representative, called a **revenue agent**. You definitely will want to consider hiring a tax pro to represent you in these circumstances.

## Strategic Moves

Generally, the agent makes an appointment to come to your business office, although the agent may go to your tax advisor's office if that's where you keep all your books and records. Here's a quick checklist to follow for a field audit:

✔ **Consult a pro** experienced in handling field audits. Although we suggested that individuals often could handle office audits on their own, we recommend seeking professional help for most field audits, especially if you're a small business owner. This type of audit involves line-by-line checks and tests to ensure you are complying with detailed tax accounting rules, as well as abiding by tax law basics by reporting all income and keeping decent records. In other words, the audit may involve technical tax issues that are well beyond your expertise. This is almost a certainty if you used paid tax preparers because your returns are relatively complex.

➤ **Observation:** These checks can be exhaustive. A professional who's been through prior field examinations can ease the process, detect weaknesses in your case and help present your side in the best possible way.

✔ **Appoint someone** within your business as a contact person for the agent—for example, your controller, tax manager or bookkeeper. Tell the IRS agent that all requests for company information (such as the minutes book, ledgers and journals) should go through the contact person. This will limit the agent's sources of information, ensure that the agent gets the facts and allow you to track the route the audit is taking.

✔ **As with an office audit,** answer only the questions you're asked. Don't volunteer information.

✔ **If the agent insists** on coming to your place of business, provide a workspace on company premises away from your employees. A revenue agent who's seen chatting with your staff is probably after more than idle gossip. He may be trying to figure out why you do things differently from others in similar businesses. At the worst, the agent may be delving into what the staff knows about your lifestyle, such as what schools your children attend, the make and model of your cars and the kind of vacations you take. The agent then would balance that information against what the company books show.

*Rule of Combat No. 13:* *Generally, you should try to arrange for the IRS agent to examine your books and other business records* ***away*** *from your place of business, such as at your accountant's or lawyer's office. Why? You don't want to give the revenue agent an opportunity to walk around and observe your operation or listen to employees. The agent may decide your business appears to be much more successful than tax returns indicate, or he may stumble across previously unidentified tax questions, which can cause you nothing but trouble.*

✔ **It's wise to ask the agent** to make all requests for information or answers at a specific time of the workday, such as in the late afternoon. Then you can provide the answers and the documents the next morning. This practice will cause the least amount of disruption to your business operation.

*Caution:* As with an office audit, make sure the agent receives only one piece of information or one document at a time. Instruct your contact person to retrieve one document ("to put back in the files") before delivering the next.

➤ **Recommendation:** Don't give the agent blanket permission to dig into your files, such as those containing canceled checks or paid bills. Also, in offering documents to the agent, make sure to remove all references to other tax years. For damage-control reasons, you want to keep the investigation tightly focused.

✔ **Make a list of all the documents** the agent reviews and the questions he asks. Also, photocopy any records the agent requests; make one copy for the agent, and keep the other for your files. These records may save you money if you decide to appeal the agent's assessment. You may be able to show that the agent had no documentary proof to support his conclusions.

✔ **Unlike an office audit,** a field audit always raises the possibility that the agent is preparing for a criminal tax case against you or your firm. This is especially true if an informant (such as a disgruntled former employee) has fingered your business by alleging operating improprieties, such as paying some employees in cash to avoid leaving paper trails. One tip-off to a possible criminal investigation: when the agent asks permission to photocopy an inordinate number of documents.

If you suspect that his real motive is to lay the groundwork for criminal proceedings, you have the right to call an immediate halt to the examination and consult your tax advisor or attorney.

## Hiring Professional Help

In deciding to have a tax pro represent you at either an office or a field audit, keep in mind the person won't gain you any special consideration from the IRS. Having a professional sit in for you at an office audit gets mixed reviews from agency personnel. Some IRS staffers say they somewhat appreciate dealing with a professional because they can avoid emotional outbursts from the taxpayer. Others may tend to give lone taxpayers attending examinations more of a break because it's their first audit and they may not be aware of recordkeeping requirements.

Only three categories of individuals are allowed to represent you in the audit process. The first consists of certified public accountants (CPAs), lawyers and Enrolled Agents. To qualify as Enrolled Agents, individuals must pass a two-day special enrollment IRS examination covering tax and tax-accounting problems. They also must submit to an extensive background investigation. Once all these requirements have been fulfilled, the IRS issues the Enrolled Agent a special numbered enrollment card. Be sure to ask to see this card from a person who claims Enrolled Agent status.

The second category consists of unenrolled tax preparers, and the third group are your employees and immediate family. "Unenrolled tax preparer" refers to the person who prepared your return for a fee and signed the return. Friends who might have prepared your return as a favor, and not for compensation, can accompany you to an examination to explain their computations, but they can't technically represent you or argue in your favor.

Only these three categories of individuals are recognized by the IRS at any stage of the audit process; *i.e.*, they're permitted to argue the tax law or the amount of tax adjustment made by the tax auditor.

*Rule of Combat No. 14: If you believe you'll end up appealing a tax auditor's adjustments, it would be wise to engage an attorney, a CPA or an Enrolled Agent. They are the only individuals permitted to practice before the IRS, which means only they can represent you beyond the examination stage of the audit process. This would include appeals made to the IRS. If you select an attorney or a CPA, make sure the person has heavy-duty tax expertise.*

## Beware 'Financial-Status Audits'

Under a relatively new IRS undertaking, auditors are being asked to compare what's shown on tax returns to what they can see, hear and dig up about you. These are known as **financial-status, economic-reality** or **lifestyle audits**—three names for the same concept.

Here we're talking about the IRS extending its longstanding office and field audit programs into new territory fraught with perils for the taxpayer.

> **Be Ready to Grant a Power of Attorney**
>
> If you decide to have an individual represent you at an audit examination and you won't be present, the IRS requires that you give the person written authorization to represent you and have access to confidential data regarding your return. Keep in mind that your tax return is considered confidential and can't be discussed with a third party unless that person has your written authorization. In most instances, authorization takes the form of a power of attorney. To grant such power in an audit process, you must fill out IRS Form 2848. *(See sample copy on page 43.)*
>
> You'll also want to keep track of your representative's progress. To do so, maintain some contact with the auditor. Insist that copies of correspondence from the IRS to your representative be forwarded to you. It's also worthwhile to contact the auditor to find out what actions she's taken concerning your case. In other words, maintain some feedback during an audit, even though you are leaving the examination up to your representative.
>
> ▶ **Observation:** If you're present during the examination, the representative doesn't need power of attorney and still can receive any confidential information the auditor requests.

For example, when a taxpayer under audit reports income of $40,000 but lives in an exclusive neighborhood, drives a new Porsche and has a big boat in the backyard, it appears to defy economic reality. Whether the auditor found this out in the course of an office or field audit doesn't really matter. The case is going to degenerate into a financial-status audit. The individual simply may have inherited a bundle, but the IRS isn't going to go away until he explains obvious discrepancies between lifestyle and reported income.

What if there are no obvious inconsistencies? Auditors are being trained to nose around and try to dig up enough "damaging" information to launch a financial-status audit. For example, in an audit of a Connecticut resident, the IRS handed the taxpayer a canned 27-question checklist asking about various financial and lifestyle matters, such as where the children went to college, how he financed personal expenses and so forth. These types of questions are clearly intended to encourage unwitting, but cooperative, citizens to supply data that the IRS will use against them. Give a few "wrong" answers, and it may take months and a ton of professional fees before the IRS admits it was barking up the wrong tree in the first place.

Thankfully, this type of behavior by the government should be a thing of the past. The IRS Restructuring and Reform Act prohibits the use of financial-status audits, except in circumstances where a "regular" audit establishes a reasonable likelihood of unreported income. In other words, financial-status audits can no longer be used as "fishing expeditions" without any real justification. Put another way, IRS personnel must now stick to auditing only the information presented on the taxpayer's return unless there are solid indications of unreported income.

The IRS Reform Act also generally requires the government to notify you in advance if it intends to contact any third parties (business associates, employees, ex-spouse, etc.) regarding your taxes. However, notification isn't required in criminal cases. Again, the intent is to force the IRS to stick to auditing items reported on your tax return, except in unusual circumstances.

## *If you're targeted ...*

Don't volunteer lifestyle information—orally or in writing. What you say can turn an audit of your tax return into an audit of *you*. Remember: You're not required to respond personally to these "off the tax return" questions until the IRS issues a summons, and that's unlikely unless the feds already suspect serious violations.

Do maintain your composure, and remember you can always get a CPA, an attorney or an Enrolled Agent to represent you in IRS matters. If you're clean, a competent tax pro often can end an unjustified financial-status investigation without too much trouble or expense.

In any case, if an IRS agent attempts to interview you about your lifestyle, simply terminate the discussion by politely saying your representative will be in touch. Get a business card from the auditor, and walk away.

*Caution:* After a nerve-racking close encounter of the financial-status kind, don't blurt out any confessions to your CPA or Enrolled Agent. However, you can tell your darkest tax secrets to an attorney. Lawyers have attorney-client privilege.

Thanks to the IRS Reform Act, CPAs and Enrolled Agents now have so-called accountant-client privilege. This means they generally don't have to reveal their communications with you (written or oral) regarding tax advice. However, they can still be forced to testify against you in criminal and corporate tax shelter cases. (Discussions and work papers used in preparation of the tax return itself aren't covered by the privilege.) Finally, note that accountant-client privilege doesn't extend to tax practitioners other than CPAs, Enrolled Agents and Enrolled Actuaries. "Unregulated" tax practitioners aren't covered except to the extent they deliver tax advice while under the supervision of a CPA, Enrolled Agent or Enrolled Actuary.

If your audit starts out as a "regular" examination and then degenerates into a criminal case, the accountant-client privilege is retroactively disallowed back to the start of the case. The broader attorney-client privilege covers you even in these matters, however.

The bottom line: Under current rules, any financial-status audit is likely to turn into a criminal case, almost by definition. So if you're targeted, talk to your attorney and keep your CPA or Enrolled Agent out of the loop. If necessary, then your attorney can hire your CPA or Enrolled Agent to help with the case. This arrangement extends the attorney-client privilege to such nonattorney advisors.

# 'Good Grief! Auditors Who Really Understand My Business'

Yet another relatively new IRS audit drive is called the Market Segment Specialization Program (MSSP). The MSSP concept involves training auditors about specific lines of business. Once its auditors understand how businesses work, they also discern all the ways taxpayers can shortchange the government.

The IRS has developed a series of MSSP audit guides for its internal training programs, covering about 40 industries, including:

- Attorneys
- Gasoline retailers
- Truckers
- Oil and gas industry
- Tobacco industry
- Entertainment industry
- Mortuaries and cemeteries
- Bed-and-breakfasts
- Air charters
- Taxicab operators
- Architects
- Barbershops and beauty salons
- Industries related to coastal and inland ports and waterways
- Music industry
- Wine industry
- Colleges and universities
- Bars and restaurants
- Mobile food vendors
- Reforestation industry
- Auto body and repair
- Pizza retailers
- Grain farmers
- Cattle auction barns
- Used car dealers
- Foreign athletes and entertainers
- Commercial fishing vessels, fish processing plants and brokers in the Alaska fishing industry

Also, the IRS has several MSSP handbooks on odd topics that only it would consider "industries":

- Golden parachutes
- Passive losses
- Rehabilitation tax credit
- Split-dollar life insurance

The MSSP guides come in varying formats, but they all highlight the relevant tax issues and give recommendations on specific audit techniques that often uncover understated income and overstated deductions.

➤ **Recommendation:** The MSSP guides are public information and are available for purchase. Consider obtaining the guide for your industry. Then consult your tax pro and conduct a "self-audit." Knowing the IRS game plan in advance, you can shore up recordkeeping weaknesses and be prepared for potential tax controversies. You can view MSSP guides online; go to **www.irs.gov/businesses/index.html** and click on Audit Techniques Guides.

The IRS has also developed a series of so-called Market Segment Understanding (MSU) documents. These deal with how specialized tax issues should be handled and have, in effect, been negotiated with representatives of affected industries. Therefore, they're considered to be "fair" to taxpayers.

MSUs cover the following:

- Tip reporting for the gaming industry
- Tip reporting for the hairstyling industry
- Farm labor noncash remuneration
- Classifying workers in the TV industry as employees or independent contractors
- Classifying limousine drivers as employees or independent contractors
- The retail liquor industry
- Garment industry contractors
- Garment manufacturers
- The commercial printing industry

Like MSSP guides, the MSU documents are useful in conducting self-audits. They're also available at **www.irs.gov/businesses/index.html** under Market Segment Understandings.

## IRS Auditor's Report: Form 4549

You will receive Form 4549 if the auditor proposes adjustments to your business tax return and you agree to the changes. *(See page 56.)* Form 4549-A (also called Income Tax Examination Changes) is used when you do not agree with all the changes.

Form 1902-B (Report of Individual Income Tax Examination Changes) is used for nonbusiness returns: in other words, for garden-variety individual Forms 1040.

Form 886-A (Explanation of Items) should accompany each of these forms, to provide explanations of the adjustment items. (Form 886-A is basically just a blank sheet that the auditor fills in.)

**Form 4549**
(Rev. May 2008)

**Department of the Treasury-Internal Revenue Service**

# Income Tax Examination Changes

Page _____ of _____

| Name and Address of Taxpayer<br>Jack and Susan Anson | Taxpayer Identification Number<br>XXX-XX-XXXX | Return Form No.:<br>1040 |
|---|---|---|
| | Person with whom examination changes were discussed. | Name and Title:<br>Jack and Susan Anson |

| 1. Adjustments to Income | Period End<br>12-31-XX | Period End<br>12-31-XX | Period End<br>12-31-XX |
|---|---|---|---|
| a. Itemized Deductions | XXXXX | XXXXX | XXXXX |
| b. Standard Deduction | | | (XXXXX) |
| c. | | | |
| d. | | | |
| e. | | | |
| f. | | | |
| g. | | | |
| h. | | | |
| i. | | | |
| j. | | | |
| k. | | | |
| l. | | | |
| m. | | | |
| n. | | | |
| o. | | | |
| p. | | | |
| 2. Total Adjustments | XXXXX | XXXXX | XXXX |
| 3. Taxable Income Per Return or as Previously Adjusted | | | |
| 4. Corrected Taxable Income<br>    Tax Method<br>    Filing Status | Tax Table<br>Joint | Tax Table<br>Joint | Tax Table<br>Joint |
| 5. Tax | | | |
| 6. Additional Taxes / Alternative Minimum Tax | | | |
| 7. Corrected Tax Liability | | | |
| 8. Less Credits  a.<br>                   b.<br>                   c.<br>                   d. | | | |
| 9. Balance *(Line 7 less Lines 8a through 8d)* | | | |
| 10. Plus Other Taxes  a.<br>                        b.<br>                        c.<br>                        d. | | | |
| 11. Total Corrected Tax Liability *(Line 9 plus Lines 10a through 10d)* | | | |
| 12. Total Tax Shown on Return or as Previously Adjusted | | | |
| 13. Adjustments to:  a.<br>                       b.<br>                       c. | | | |
| 14. Deficiency-Increase in Tax or *(Overassessment-Decrease in Tax)*<br>*(Line 11 less Line 12 adjusted by Lines 13a through 13c)* | | | |
| 15. Adjustments to Prepayment Credits - Increase *(Decrease)* | | | |
| 16. Balance Due or *(Overpayment)* - *(Line 14 adjusted by Line 15)*<br>*(Excluding interest and penalties)* | XXXX.XX | XXXX.XX | XXX.XX |

The Internal Revenue Service has agreements with state tax agencies under which information about federal tax, including increases or decreases, is exchanged with the states. If this change affects the amount of your state income tax, you should amend your state return by filing the necessary forms.

You may be subject to backup withholding if you underreport your interest, dividend, or patronage dividend income you earned and do not pay the required tax. The IRS may order backup withholding *(withholding of a percentage of your dividend and/or interest income)* if the tax remains unpaid after it has been assessed and four notices have been issued to you over a 120-day period.

Catalog Number 23105A         www.irs.gov         Form **4549** (Rev. 5-2008)

| Form **4549** (Rev. May 2008) | Department of the Treasury-Internal Revenue Service<br>**Income Tax Examination Changes** | | Page_____ of _____ |
|---|---|---|---|
| Name of Taxpayer<br>Jack and Susan Anson | | Taxpayer Identification Number<br>XXX-XX-XXXX | Return Form No.:<br>1040 |

| 17. Penalties/ Code Sections | Period End<br>12-31-XX | Period End<br>12-31-XX | Period End<br>12-31-XX |
|---|---|---|---|
| a. Accuracy Related Penalty - IRC 6662 | XXX.XX | XXX.XX | XX.XX |
| b. | | | |
| c. | | | |
| d. | | | |
| e. | | | |
| f. | | | |
| g. | | | |
| h. | | | |
| i. | | | |
| j. | | | |
| k. | | | |
| l. | | | |
| m. | | | |
| n. | | | |
| 18. Total Penalties | | | |
| Underpayment attributable to negligence: *(1981-1987)* *A tax addition of 50 percent of the interest due on the underpayment will accrue until it is paid or assessed.* | | | |
| Underpayment attributable to fraud: *(1981-1987)* *A tax addition of 50 percent of the interest due on the underpayment will accrue until it is paid or assessed.* | | | |
| Underpayment attributable to Tax Motivated Transactions *(TMT)*. The interest will accrue and be assessed at 120% of the under- payment rate in accordance with IRC §6621(c) | | | |
| 19. Summary of Taxes, Penalties and Interest: | | | |
| a. Balance due or *(Overpayment)* Taxes - *(Line 16, Page 1)* | XXXX.XX | XXXX.XX | XXX.XX |
| b. Penalties *(Line 18)* - computed to | XXX.XX | XXX.XX | XX.XX |
| c. Interest *(IRC § 6601)* - computed to | XXX.XX | XXX.XX | XX.XX |
| d. TMT Interest - computed to    *(on TMT underpayment)* | | | |
| e. Amount due or *(refund)* - *(sum of Lines a, b, c and d)* | XXXX.XX | XXXX.XX | XXXX.XX |

Other Information:

| Examiner's Signature: | Employee ID:<br>XXXXXXX | Office:<br>SBSE- Exam | Date:<br>XX-XX-XXXX |
|---|---|---|---|

Consent to Assessment and Collection- I do not wish to exercise my appeal rights with the Internal Revenue Service or to contest in the United States Tax Court the findings in this report. Therefore, I give my consent to the immediate assessment and collection of any increase in tax and penalties, and accept any decrease in tax and penalties shown above, plus additional interest as provided by law. It is understood that this report is subject to acceptance by the Area Director, Area Manager, Specialty Tax Program Chief, or Director of Field Operations.

**PLEASE NOTE:** *If a joint return was filed, BOTH taxpayers must sign*

| Signature of Taxpayer | Date: | Signature of Taxpayer | Date: |
|---|---|---|---|
| By: | | Title: | Date: |

Catalog Number 23105A          www.irs.gov          Form **4549** (Rev. 5-2008)

# WINNING AFTER LOSING A BATTLE 9

Despite all your hard work in amassing receipts for your defense before the IRS, don't be surprised if you're hit with adjustments. Only about 20% of audits produce "no change" decisions, in which the IRS has accepted your return as you filed it. The remainder of audits result in an auditor's proposed adjustments. You may agree to all, some or none of them. That's your right, but be sure you reach a practical decision.

## Assess Your Options

The climax of any audit comes at the end, when the auditor has reviewed all your records and has answered all your questions. (In the case of a field audit, the revenue agent completes the examination and then sets up a closing conference, where he will discuss the issues and the adjustments.) An audit report will explain the changes in your return, along with the new tax or refund *(see page 55)*.

Let's assume the auditor proposes adjustments to your return, requiring you to pay additional taxes. Should you agree to pay?

The answer depends on the type of adjustments. You may have to pay only a token tax, perhaps far less than expected. You may even breathe a sigh of relief that the auditor hasn't uncovered other deficiencies that you feared might show up. This is especially true in a field audit, in which the general rule is to settle the case at the lowest level to save your business more expense and to keep the agent from discovering other issues. When you weigh all these factors, it may be wise to pay up and have the case closed. From the standpoint of timing, you'll have 30 days from the date you receive the audit report to decide what action to take.

Suppose you decide to take this course and you do agree with the adjustments. About 20 days after receiving the audit report, you will be sent a reminder, along with Form 870, the Waiver of Restrictions on Assessment and Collection of Deficiency in Tax and Acceptance of Overassessment *(see sample on page 64)*. That's a

---

***Rule of Combat No. 15:*** *Be aware that if you do sign Form 870, you forfeit your opportunity to appeal to the U.S. Tax Court. The Tax Court can hear only cases in which the IRS has issued a Notice of Deficiency. If you waived the notice by signing Form 870, the Tax Court, in effect, loses jurisdiction over your case. You still can initiate a suit in the U.S. Court of Federal Claims or a U.S. District Court, but you'll have to pay the assessed amount first and then get a refund if you win your case. Moreover, filing suit would permit the IRS to claim that additional tax is owed, so a court suit may become a double-edged sword.*

mouthful, but it's significant: The IRS requires you to sign the form before it can proceed to assess and collect any additional tax. Under the Internal Revenue Code, a taxpayer can't be assessed without the IRS issuing a statutory Notice of Deficiency. By signing Form 870, you, the taxpayer, simply waive the required Notice of Deficiency (basically a billing statement for the taxes, penalties and interest) so that the IRS can assess and then collect the deficient tax. The Notice of Deficiency is often referred to as the 90-Day Letter.

Form 870 will show the type of tax involved, along with the taxable years covered, the amount of the deficiency and applicable penalties.

## If You Disagree With the Adjustments ...

Suppose that you don't sign Form 870. In fact, during the final session with the tax auditor, in which adjustments are presented, you decide to disagree on the merit of any or all of them.

Make the auditor go through each issue, and check whether the figures are added properly. Review the data that support deductions, exemptions, etc. You might try doing this while the IRS staffer goes over the return. In this way, you tend to force her into a decision, thereby making it difficult for her to increase the adjustments later.

At this point of the audit process you should try negotiation. You have a few factors going for you.

First, the auditor is under pressure to close your case as quickly as possible. To thwart the IRS, you can throw in a few obstacles. If you're appearing alone at the audit and remain dogged about a certain adjustment, for example, you can threaten to bring in your accountant to prove your point. IRS employees are only human, after all, and probably won't relish going over the same old tax trail with your accountant. This may lead to a compromise.

Second, if you suspect that it's going to be tough to prove some of the issues raised, be prepared by bringing along a few deductions that you just happened to forget to include in your return. (For example, you may have forgone home-office deductions because you were afraid they would trigger an audit. Obviously, you have nothing to lose by claiming those write-offs now.) This is a legal maneuver you can use to offset some of the additional tax you might have to pay. Make sure, however, that you have sufficient documentation along to back up those deductions.

**Rule of Combat No. 16:** *You have every right to question the auditor or agent on all adjustments. It may be that he or she generalized in setting the adjustment amounts. Now's the time to find out what the auditor's strong and weak points are in regard to your return. This knowledge will come in handy at a later date if you decide to appeal the finding.*

Third, if you reach an impasse in arguing your points, and the auditor refuses to change her mind about the adjustments, you can always ask to see her supervisor. Since this means the clock will still be ticking on your case, the IRS representative may agree to meet you halfway on the adjustments.

## To Appeal or Not to Appeal ...

If you totally disagree with the audit report and can't resolve matters with the IRS personnel you've been dealing with, you have some alternatives. You might ask the Appeals Office of the IRS to take a look at the case, or you could go directly to Tax Court. By law, the IRS is now required to enclose a booklet explaining your appeal rights with any Notice of Deficiency *(see page 65)* sent to you.

You have 30 days from the time you receive the audit report to decide on your next step. Don't sit on your decision: The IRS is serious about wanting an answer within 30 days. If you don't respond, your case goes into the "unagreed" file at the IRS, and then you're restricted to arguing your case in the Tax Court.

*Rule of Combat No. 17: If you still want to fight, but without going to court, let the IRS know that you want to make an administrative appeal to a higher level within the agency.*

The administrative appeal route is open to you only after the audit report has been written and sent to you. This course gives you another chance to argue your points before an experienced IRS examiner or appeals officer. Chances are the examiner will spot an unfair adjustment and correct it to your advantage. If you should lose at the appeals level, then you can go to Tax Court.

*Caution:* You take a risk in asking for an administrative appeal. The process gives the IRS another crack at your return. Although the appeals examiner is obligated under the agency's rules to consider the issues covered in the audit report, he also may uncover issues that went undetected during the audit. Those issues could result in a major tax liability for you. So, weigh this disadvantage against the chance of arguing your case again.

In reviewing the audit report, you or your accountant may discover that the IRS auditor didn't spot a major issue that, by itself, could result in a substantial tax adjustment. Needless to say, you don't want to risk an appeals officer finding it, and so you would decide against an administrative appeal and consider taking your case directly to Tax Court.

## How to Appeal

If you're confident that no additional issues will be uncovered, you can start the appeals process by lodging a protest with your IRS district office within 30 days after receiving the audit report. In your correspondence, spell out the adjustments that you're protesting, together with the additional tax dollar amount the auditor is proposing and the tax years involved. Also state your argument, along with the points that support your case, including citations from the Internal Revenue Code.

Follow the guidelines in IRS Publication 5, entitled *Your Appeal Rights and How to Prepare a Protest If You Don't Agree.* You should have received this with your Notice of Deficiency. If not, ask the auditor for a copy.

In appealing a field audit, you must send a formal protest letter when the proposed additional tax exceeds $10,000. You need to make an oral protest only on amounts of $2,500 or less. For totals between $2,500 and $10,000, a written protest is optional; however, you must send a brief written statement of the issues in dispute.

Upon receiving your protest letter, the IRS assigns it to the Appeals Office. An appointment letter, stating the time and place for the appeals session, is then sent to you. This second meeting with the IRS may not necessarily take place in the same office in which you were audited.

▶ **Recommendation:** If you're appealing a field audit on your business, it would be wise to have both your accountant and lawyer attend the appeals proceedings.

It may turn out that the appeals process will involve more than one meeting. You can furnish the IRS with more information at this stage. However, refrain from submitting it until after your first meeting with the appeals officer. You don't want to give the government any facts or unveil any legal theory until you learn the position of the government or, in this case, the appeals officer.

When attending the appeals session, your attitude should be the same as it was during the audit process. In other words, be on time and treat the appeals officer in a professional manner, even though you may be seething about the adjustments proposed. You'll find that appeals officers generally have undergone long service and training within the IRS and are very knowledgeable.

## *What's so appealing?*

Taking the appeals route has a number of advantages for you. First, the appeals officer, who functions almost like an administrative judge, can rely only on the written explanations in the audit report to press the IRS' position. If the explanations in the audit report happen to be incomplete, the appeals officer could throw out the adjustments and rule in your favor. For example, the auditor might have ruled out your deductions for two reasons but listed only one reason in his written report. In this case, all you would have to do to get a favorable ruling from the appeals officer is to counter that one listed reason.

Second, the appeals officer has more leeway to settle a case than the person who conducted the audit. The appeals examiner obviously is looking to make you pay the correct amount of tax, but he also wants to keep you from going to Tax Court. In plain language, the appeals officer can wheel and deal, and he will make concessions in your favor if he believes the adjustments might be hard to prove in Tax Court. The examiner also looks to save the IRS the money and the inconvenience of going to court.

Third, you'll find that the appeals officer, being the final IRS authority over most tax cases, is permitted to be more receptive to oral testimony as proof of the taxpayer's points than the auditor was.

What most people don't realize is that you, as the taxpayer, must initiate any settlement proposal to the appeals officer. Prior to that first meeting, calculate a low offer—one that you would gladly accept—and a high offer beyond which you would not go. You might have an accountant do the math. Generally, the appeals officer already has made similar calculations before meeting with you.

At some juncture in the proceedings, you will sense that the time is right for some type of settlement. You should be ready to accept the deal if it falls within your settlement parameters.

▶ **Observation:** Chances are you'll come out of an appeals session owing less tax than when you went in. *Exception:* When your case involves an issue that the IRS has decided to make a national example of (for instance, underreported income by well-known entertainers or athletes), you should expect no concessions. In these instances, the appeals officer will refer any settlement decisions to the Office of the District Counsel. If the case can't be settled at this level, chances are it will end up in Tax Court.

### *Case closed*

Let's assume you're satisfied with the appeals officer's finding, and you want to close your case once and for all. You can do this by requesting either a Form 870-AD or a final closing agreement from the IRS.

Form 870-AD is the special waiver form used by the IRS Appeals Office that prohibits the taxpayer from filing a claim for a refund or a credit for the tax years involved in the audit. In return, the IRS agrees not to reopen the case in the absence of such factors as fraud, malfeasance, misrepresentation of fact or major mathematical errors.

You can secure even greater finality with a **closing agreement**. It's generally irrevocable and can be set aside only by a finding of fraud, malfeasance or misrepresentation of fact. Also, it's the responsibility of the party seeking to set aside such an agreement to prove that fraud, malfeasance or misrepresentation of fact has occurred.

While statistics show that the Appeals Office settles about 84% of the audit disputes it takes on, you may find yourself among the 16% who must decide whether they want to go to U.S. Tax Court with their grievances.

## Form 870: Waiver of Restrictions

If you agree to the auditor's adjustments, you may save on interest owed by signing Form 870 *(see sample on page 64)*. It allows the IRS to assess and collect the additional tax owed without first issuing a Notice of Deficiency *(see sample on page 65)*.

Remember that by signing this form, you forfeit your opportunity to appeal your case to the Tax Court.

Form **870**
(Rev. March 1992)

Department of the Treasury—Internal Revenue Service

# Waiver of Restrictions on Assessment and Collection of Deficiency in Tax and Acceptance of Overassessment

Date received by Internal Revenue Service

Names and address of taxpayers *(Number, street, city or town, State, ZIP code)*

Social security or employer identification number

## Increase (Decrease) in Tax and Penalties

| Tax year ended | Tax | Penalties |||
|---|---|---|---|---|
| | | | | |
| | | | | |
| | | | | |
| | | | | |
| | | | | |
| | | | | |
| | | | | |
| | | | | |

(For instructions, see back of form)

**Consent to Assessment and Collection**

I consent to the immediate assessment and collection of any deficiencies *(increase in tax and penalties)* and accept any overassessment *(decrease in tax and penalties)* shown above, plus any interest provided by law. I understand that by signing this waiver, I will not be able to contest these years in the United States Tax Court, unless additional deficiencies are determined for these years.

| | | Date |
|---|---|---|
| **YOUR SIGNATURE HERE** → | | |
| **SPOUSE'S SIGNATURE** → | | Date |
| **TAXPAYER'S REPRESENTATIVE HERE** → | | Date |
| **CORPORATE NAME** → | | |
| **CORPORATE OFFICER(S) SIGN HERE** → | Title | Date |
| | Title | Date |

Catalog Number 16894U

Form **870** (Rev. 3-1992)

# The 90-Day Letter: Notice of Deficiency

This letter represents your formal Notice of Deficiency (in other words, that you owe additional tax as far as the IRS is concerned). The letter gives you 90 days to decide to fight by filing a petition with the Tax Court—thus the name.

---

Internal Revenue Service　　　　　Department of the Treasury
District Director

CERTIFIED MAIL

Date:　　　　　　　　　　　　　　Social Security or Employer
　　　　　　　　　　　　　　　　　Identification Number:

　　　　　　　　　　　　　　　　　Tax Year Ended and Deficiency:
　　　　　　　　　　　　　　　　　See Below
　　　　　　　　　　　　　　　　　Person to Contact:

　　　　　　　　　　　　　　　　　Contact Telephone Number:

Dear _____:

　　We have determined that there is a deficiency (increase) in your income tax as shown above. This letter is a NOTICE OF DEFICIENCY sent to you as required by law. The enclosed statement shows how we figured the deficiency.

　　If you want to contest this deficiency in court before making any payment, you have 90 days from the above mailing date of this letter (150 days if addressed to you outside of the United States) to file a petition with the United States Tax Court for a redetermination of the deficiency. To secure the petition form, write to United States Tax Court, 400 Second Street, NW, Washington, D.C. 20217. The completed petition form, together with a copy of this letter, must be returned to the same address and received within 90 days from the above mailing date (150 days if addressed to you outside of the United States).

　　The time in which you must file a petition with the court (90 or 150 days as the case may be) is fixed by law and the Court cannot consider your case if your petition is filed late. If this letter is addressed to both a husband and wife, and both want to petition the Tax Court, both must sign the petition or each must file a separate, signed petition.

　　If you dispute not more than $50,000 for any one tax year, a simplified procedure is provided by the Tax Court for small tax cases. You can get information about this procedure, as well as a petition form you can use, by writing to the Clerk of the United States Tax Court at 400 Second Street, NW, Washington, D.C. 20217. You should do this promptly if you intend to file a petition with the Tax Court.

　　You may represent yourself before the Tax Court, or you may be represented by anyone admitted to practice before the Court. If you decide not to file a petition with the Tax Court, we would appreciate it if you would sign and return the enclosed waiver form. This will permit us to assess the deficiency quickly and will limit the accumulation of interest. The enclosed envelope is for your convenience. If you decide not to sign and return the statement and you do not timely petition the Tax Court, the law requires us to assess and bill you for the deficiency after 90 days from the above mailing date of this letter (150 days if this letter is addressed to you outside the United States).

　　If you are a "C" corporation, this letter may invoke an interest rate 2% higher than the normal rate of interest, computed on the amount finally determined due, as provided by Section 6621(c) of the Internal Revenue Code.

　　　　　　　　　　　　　　　　　　　　　　　Letter 531 (DO) (1-87)

---

*(continued on next page)*

*(continued from page 65)*

> If you have questions about this letter, please write to the person whose name and address are shown on this letter. If you write, please attach this letter to help identify your account. Keep the copy for your records. Also, please include your telephone number and the most convenient time for us to call, so we can contact you if we need additional information.
>
> If you prefer, you may call the IRS contact person at the number shown above. If this number is outside your local calling area, there will be a long-distance charge to you.
>
> You may call the IRS telephone number listed in your local directory. An IRS employee there may be able to help you, but the contact person at the address shown on this letter is most familiar with your case.
>
> Thank you for your cooperation.
>
>                                   Sincerely yours,
>
>                                   Commissioner
>
>                                   District Director
>
> Enclosures:
> Copy of this letter
> Statement
> Envelope
>
> Tax Year Ended and Deficiency
>
>                                   Penalty
>                              Addition to Tax Under
>                               Internal Revenue Code
>                                   Section
>
>                                   Letter 531 (DO) (1-87)

# Taking the IRS to Court

# 10

Here's another scenario you might consider in your battle with the IRS. At the time your audit report was completed and forwarded to you, you had 30 days to file for an administrative appeal within the IRS.

At that time, however, you could have forgone sending the letter of protest to the IRS and simply awaited your Notice of Deficiency, or "90-Day Letter." As we've said, this notice simply informs you of the amount of tax due, the reasons the additional tax is due and that you have 90 days to file a petition with the U.S. Tax Court. If you don't file a petition within that 90-day period, you can expect to receive a bill from the IRS.

Suppose you decide to file a petition within the 90 days. (Don't count this period as merely being three months—it's literally 90 days.) Because you have filed a petition, you don't have to pay the tax until your case is resolved in the U.S. Tax Court. However, keep in mind that interest will accrue on the unpaid taxes, and if you lose, you're liable for both interest and the tax amount.

*Rule of Combat No. 18:* Paying the tax before you go to court won't hurt your case, and it will limit your liability if you lose. Even though you decide to go directly to the Tax Court for a resolution, you won't lose your opportunity for an administrative appeal within the IRS. Your case will be referred to the Appeals Office for settlement after it's been docketed in the court.

To recap, then, once you receive your audit report, you have two options:

**1.** You can file for an administrative appeal within the IRS, and then, assuming you don't reach an agreement, you can petition the Tax Court for redress.

**2.** You can petition the Tax Court immediately after your final audit and have the court refer your case to the Appeals Office of the IRS for settlement. Realize, however, that you must ask for and receive a Notice of Deficiency before seeking a Tax Court hearing. So if you know you want to go to court, you may want to ask for a deficiency notice immediately to speed up the process.

During the period in which you are deciding whether to take your case to Tax Court, the IRS will give you another crack at settlement: It will allow you to present to its auditor or appeals officer any new data or documents that might alter the agency's finding.

## Petitioning the Tax Court

The Tax Court was formed solely to hear tax cases in nearly 80 cities throughout the United States. It is particularly advantageous to the small taxpayer because it doesn't require going to the expense of hiring a lawyer. You would be well advised to retain a lawyer, though, if your case will be heard as a regular, as opposed to a "small-case," court procedure *(see below)*.

➤ **Recommendation:** If you do hire an attorney, make sure the person has been admitted to practice before the Tax Court.

Two procedures are available through the Tax Court. If your case involves a disputed tax of $50,000 or less, you may elect a **small-case tax procedure**. This type of hearing is considerably less formal than a regular hearing, in that the rules of evidence are less strict and the formal trial practices are eased. You probably won't need a lawyer for a small-case procedure, and there's usually no need to prepare written briefs for the judge. The **regular procedure** is more complex and may involve weighty legal exchanges.

In both types of procedures, your arguments are heard only by a judge; there aren't any juries in Tax Court proceedings.

To initiate either Tax Court procedure, you have to file a petition within 90 days after receiving your Notice of Deficiency from the IRS. You can secure a petition form by calling the clerk of the court, U.S. Tax Court, in Washington, D.C. at (202) 521-0700 or online at **www.ustaxcourt.gov/forms.htm**.

*Note:* You must specifically elect the small-case procedure by filing so-called Form 2; otherwise the regular procedure will apply. Include all the issues, as well as your arguments, on your petition. To file:

♦ Attach a copy of your Notice of Deficiency to the original copy of the petition.
♦ Besides the original, include two photocopies of the petition when requesting the small-case procedure, or four copies when electing the regular procedure.
♦ Include Form 4 (on which you state your preferences as to the place of the trial).
♦ Attach the nominal filing fee, which you can pay by check or money order.

Because the petition must be received within 90 days of the time you received your deficiency notice, it's advisable to send the Tax Court petition and additional required materials by certified mail, return receipt requested.

Assuming, then, that the Tax Court receives your petition within the stipulated time, a copy of it is sent to the IRS commissioner. In a regular—as opposed to a small-case—procedure the commissioner's office has 60 days to file a formal answer to the petition, or 45 days to file a motion in the case. The formal answer from the IRS must admit or deny each allegation you raised in your petition. Once the commissioner's office files its answer, you have 45 days to file your response, in which you must admit or deny the commissioner's material facts. You also have 30 days to file motions on the answer.

➤ **Observation:** This formal exchange isn't required, however, in the small-case procedure unless the Tax Court or the IRS specifically demands an answer to a question about your petition.

## The Pros and Cons of Tax Court

If you go to Tax Court, you don't have to pay the disputed tax, interest and penalties beforehand. Because the court is a separate entity from the IRS, your case also receives an impartial hearing—a fresh look from judges who don't always agree with the IRS' interpretation of the Internal Revenue Code.

➤ **Observation:** With the less formal small-case procedure you're also allowed to introduce favorable points that wouldn't be permitted under the regular procedure. In addition, you save some time: A regular procedure may take one to three years; a small-case procedure, six months to a year.

On the downside: Going to Tax Court exposes you to the risk of additional tax because the judges review not only all the IRS evidence but also the documents you present at the hearing. In other words, they look at your entire tax liability for the year in question. This means that, similar to the administrative appeals procedure, you risk the Tax Court's uncovering certain issues that went unnoticed during the audit process.

In a small-case procedure there's another disadvantage: Once the Tax Court rules, the decision is final, and you can't appeal. In the more formal regular procedure you can appeal to the U.S. Court of Appeals for the circuit in which you live. You have 90 days to file this type of appeal. After the Court of Appeals, your last legal recourse remains the U.S. Supreme Court.

*Caution:* If you decide to appeal the Tax Court's ruling, the IRS can assess and collect the tax it won unless you post a bond before filing your appeal to the higher court.

## Other Legal Recourses

Other than Tax Court, you have two options for appealing an audit assessment: the U.S. District Court and the U.S. Court of Federal Claims. Before you can go to either of these, you must pay the amount of taxes in question and file for a refund, stating your specific grounds for claiming one. You must make the claim within three years from the time the return was filed, or two years after the time the tax was paid, whichever is later. If your claim is rejected or you don't get an answer to your filing within six months, you can sue.

In District Court, you can have a jury trial, which isn't possible in Tax Court or Claims Court. Other than the right to be heard by a jury, the reason to pick one court over another comes down to how you want to use legal precedent.

A District Court is bound by a previous decision of the Court of Appeals of that circuit. The Court of Federal Claims is bound by prior decisions of the Court of Appeals for the Federal Circuit.

So your choice of the arena could come down to the one in which past cases appear to favor your situation.

## To the Winner Belong Some Spoils

If you do take the IRS to court and win, you may be able to recover your legal expenses. The same is true even if you lose, provided you made the IRS an earlier settlement offer for more than what the court determined you owe.

Recoverable expenses can include court costs; the expense of expert witnesses; and the cost of any study, test or report necessary to prepare your case.

If the case was heard in Tax Court, you can recover fees paid to anyone authorized to practice there. Generally, however, you can't recover an attorney's fee that exceeds $125 an hour (adjusted annually for inflation) unless special factors justify a higher fee.

To be the winner in recovering any fees, the "prevailing party" must:

♦ Establish that the IRS' position was not substantially justified.
♦ Prevail substantially, either on the amount in question or on one significant issue, or have offered (in writing) to settle for more than the court-determined amount within 30 days before the case is set for trial.
♦ Meet a financial eligibility test. Any individual whose net worth exceeds $2 million at the time litigation begins isn't eligible. A business isn't eligible if its net worth exceeds $7 million or it has more than 500 workers.

# If You Lose the War

# 11

Let's assume that you lose your hard-fought battle with the IRS, and it's time to pay up. First, you will get a bill from the IRS that contains the balance of tax due, plus interest. If you're really unlucky, the IRS also will tack on penalties. The interest on the additional tax balance is figured from the date your return was due to the date when the IRS receives your signed audit report or waiver of restrictions.

The interest rates for the underpayment of taxes can vary from quarter to quarter. They're actually low compared to what you would pay on credit card debt or an unsecured line of credit.

*Rule of Combat No. 19:* *You can avoid the accrual of additional interest on unpaid tax by paying the estimated amount of your deficiency prior to your audit examination. You would take this course only if you believed that the audit would result in your owing additional tax.*

## If You Don't Have the Money

If you can't swing the entire payment of the tax, first try to pay off what you owe in installments. Individual taxpayers can do this by filing Form 9465 (Installment Agreement Request). The IRS will automatically agree with any proposed payment program in which the amount owed by an individual is less than $10,000 and the proposed repayment period is 36 months or less.

For bigger amounts or longer repayment terms, the IRS will ask you to fill out some forms that amount to a personal financial statement. Lately, the agency has demonstrated an admirable willingness to cooperate with taxpayers who "fess up" to what they owe and are trying their best to pay off the liability.

## Can You Expect a Repeat Audit?

IRS policy is supposed to minimize repetitive audits of nonbusiness returns when you've been audited within the last two years and had little or no change in your tax bill. So if you receive a letter scheduling an audit of identical items that the IRS examined in either of the preceding two years, have the auditor review the returns. If the items were checked in that period, the auditor can end the audit and you're off the hook.

Remember, though, there's no restriction on audits of issues of a "nonrecurring" nature that were audited previously and left unchanged.

### Will Using a Tax Advisor Absolve Your Penalty Sins?

Even though the tax law typically presumes that you—not your preparer—are responsible for your return, one of the best defenses against IRS penalties is to show that you relied on the advice of a competent tax professional.

Although each case turns on its own merit, the general rule of thumb says you won't have to pay the usual tax penalties, but you're still liable for any underpayments.

**Case in point:** An Illinois taxpayer took an early 401(k) distribution but failed to report the appropriate 10% penalty tax on his return. He claimed that he was unsophisticated about tax matters and had relied on a tax professional to prepare his return.

Since the taxpayer had acted in good faith, the Tax Court said he didn't have to pay an accuracy-related penalty. *(Glenn, TC Summary Opinion 2005-127)*

On the other hand, you can't expect to dodge tax liability altogether. The general rule: The return you file is your obligation.

**No late-filing forgiveness.** The IRS and courts rarely give you a break on late-filing penalties when you blame your tax preparer for the tardiness. If you're concerned about this, ask your tax preparer to give you the return to mail (or request a confirmation of the online filing). That way, you'll know it went out on time.

## Three Ways to Escape IRS Penalties

When it comes to avoiding IRS penalties, the best offense is a good defense: Avoid being assessed penalties in the first place. Here are three key steps:

**1. Hire a competent tax pro.** Hopefully, a professional will give you lots of valuable tax-saving advice. But even more important: Having a tax pro on your side is highly recommended when things turn ugly.

**2. Stay away from the bad seeds.** When tax professionals take outrageous or unfounded tax return positions on behalf of their clients, they can land on the IRS "problem preparer" list. Their clients are likely to be audited more frequently than those of other tax return preparers. At worst, the IRS auditor will be suspicious of your return from the get-go.

**3. Keep your tax specialist in the loop.** How can you expect good advice if you don't provide all the necessary facts and figures? Keep your tax professional updated on your situation. The tax law presumes that you—not your tax return preparer—are ultimately responsible for your return.